THE ECONOMICS OF ARMS

The Economics of Big Business

This series of books provides short, accessible introductions to the economics of major business sectors. Each book focuses on one particular global industry and examines its business model, economic strategy, the determinants of profitability as well as the unique issues facing its economic future. More general cross-sector challenges, which may be ethical, technological or environmental, as well as wider questions raised by the concentration of economic power, are also explored. The series offers rigorous presentations of the fundamental economics underpinning key industries suitable for both course use and a professional readership.

Published

The Economics of Music
Peter Tschmuck

The Economics of Arms
Keith Hartley

The Economics of Airlines
Volodymyr Bilotkach

THE ECONOMICS OF ARMS

KEITH HARTLEY

agenda
publishing

To my wife, Winifred, and our family:
  Adam, Rachel, Oliver and Imogen Hartley
  Professor Lucy Hartley
  Dr Cecilia and Martyn, Matthew Jacob,
    Kathryn Olivia and Sophie Elizabeth Ellis

© Keith Hartley 2017

First published in 2017 by Agenda Publishing

Agenda Publishing Limited
The Core
Science Central
Bath Lane
Newcastle upon Tyne
NE4 5TF
www.agendapub.com

ISBN 978-1-911116-23-3 (hardcover)
ISBN 978-1-911116-24-0 (paperback)

British Library Cataloguing-in-Publication Data
A catalogue record for this book is available from the British Library

Typeset by T&T Productions Ltd, London
Printed and bound in the UK by CPI Group (UK) Ltd, Croydon, CR0 4YY

CONTENTS

PREFACE

Why this book? I was attracted by the idea of a relatively short book on the economics of the arms industry. Economics has a contribution to make to the understanding of an industry that is often the subject of criticism and condemnation. It is an industry in which economics, morality and ethics cannot be avoided. Such a combination provides massive opportunities for economists to contribute to the debate by identifying myths, emotion and special pleading, and subjecting these to economic scrutiny and critical evaluation. This book brings together my research interests in arms industries; it presents an economic analysis and evaluation of the industry; and it attempts to inform readers about this controversial industry, which is so important for the future of civilization. Effectively, the book tells you all you need to know, and more, about the economics of the arms industry.

This book reflects a lifetime of interest in arms industries. I was born in Leeds on 14 July 1940 in the early stages of the Battle of Britain (officially the battle started on 10 July 1940) and my date of birth coincided with the anniversary of the French Revolution and the storming of the Bastille (14 July 1789). My parents worked in the clothing industry and my father also served in the Royal Air Force (RAF). My early life was dominated by the exploits of Spitfires, Hurricanes, Lancasters, Halifaxes and Mosquitos. The first jet fighter aircraft entered RAF service in 1944 and the jet engine revolutionized air warfare and civilian air travel. I followed these developments by attending annual Battle of Britain air displays at nearby RAF Church

Fenton (now East Leeds Airport) and RAF Finningley (now Robin Hood Airport). I often cycled to the local RAF bases, as well as visiting disused former bomber bases. My interest in military history and former RAF bases has continued to this day, and I recently discovered a Mosquito base in Norfolk with the delightful name of Little Snoring, the exploits of which are recorded in the local church.

The economics came later. I started studying economics by accident: my sixth-form subject preferences could not be fitted into the school timetable so I had to choose a third A level. My sixth-form tutor taught economics and he persuaded me to take the subject for A level. This was the start of my eventual academic career. I studied economics at Hull University and on graduation I was offered a grant to study for a PhD. My fascination with aircraft meant that my choice of PhD topic had to be the economics of the UK aircraft industry. This brought me into contact with some of the leading names in the industry, such as Sir Sydney Camm (designer of the Hurricane fighter aircraft), Sir George Edwards (leading British aircraft designer and industrialist) and Aubrey Jones (Minister of Supply, 1957–9). One leading economics professor gave me some unhelpful advice, asserting that there "was not a PhD in the aircraft industry". I was awarded my PhD by publication in 1974: the University of Hull allowed PhDs by publication so I avoided the tedium and grind of writing a conventional lengthy thesis to be read by no one.

The next stage in my career was undertaken at the new University of York, where I arrived in 1964. Here, I was greatly influenced by the academic leadership shown by Alan Peacock and Jack Wiseman. Alan Peacock encouraged staff to publish while Jack Wiseman supported my research ideas. My interest in the aircraft industry developed into an interest in defence and a desire to establish defence economics as an acceptable part of the discipline of economics. In 1977 I was awarded a NATO Research Fellowship that enabled me to visit the Pentagon, major US aircraft firms and the Rand Corporation. The fellowship was extended to include European aircraft firms and led to the book *NATO Arms Co-operation* (London: Allen & Unwin, 1982).

My research in defence economics has focused on industry studies, procurement policy and international collaboration. Examples include project case studies of the Eurofighter Typhoon, the Challenger main battle tank, the Warrior Armoured Fighting Vehicle, the Bowman communication system, the Hercules replacement (the Future Large Aircraft, which later became the A400M Airlifter), the UK aircraft carrier, the Astute submarine and the Trident replacement. I was involved in Ministry of Defence studies of defence exports, valuing defence output and the UK profit rules on non-competitive contracts. A European Commission study extended my research interests to Europe and the economic benefits of a Single Market for Defence Equipment. A UN study further developed my research into the economic aspects of disarmament (1993). Being adviser to the House of Commons Defence Committee also extended my interests into different and topical aspects of defence policy (e.g., defence budgets and major procurement projects).

My research interests in defence economics were reflected in two further initiatives.

First, in 1990, I created the Centre for Defence Economics at the University of York, which remained in existence until my retirement from the university in 2007. The centre specialized in research and consultancy in defence economics with projects funded by research councils, government departments, the European Commission, the European Defence Agency, the UN and industry.

Second, also in 1990, I helped to create a new academic journal, namely, *Defence Economics* (with Todd Sandler as North American editor). The journal was initially published four times a year, but this has since increased to six times a year and the journal has been renamed *Defence and Peace Economics*. It is now an established academic journal with worldwide contributions (US academics dominated the early contributions).

Writing a book on the economics of arms industries, one cannot avoid the moral dimension. My position on arms industries is that they are justified for self-defence against external aggression and that there are just wars. I regard the Second World War as a just war fought by the Allies to prevent a military dictatorship by Hitler's Nazi Germany, with its forceful occupation of Europe, the holocaust and the deprivation of its citizens of their lives, freedoms and liberties. My long-term hope is for a peaceful world where international disputes are settled by peaceful methods rather than by conflict. Nor do I have any qualms about studying the efficiency of arms industries. Improvements in the efficiency of arms industries releases scarce resources for alternative uses, such as building more houses, hospitals and schools, or lowering taxation. Inefficiency in any part of the public or private sector of an economy, and not just in the arms industry, is socially unacceptable. Nor does improved efficiency in arms industries lead to wars. In fact, inefficiency in arms industries is more likely to result in conflict: it means that a nation will be poorly armed and vulnerable to attack. My task is to show how economists can apply their models and analysis to arms industries, thereby contributing to greater understanding of the industry and its role and importance in an economy.

My explanation of the economics of arms industries is based on my view that economics should be readable and understandable by non-specialists and should have something useful to say about the real world. Empirical testing of theories against real-world data should be a basic requirement of the profession. Sadly, the requirements of the UK University Research Assessment Exercises have taken the economics profession in directions which are measurable but not desirable for economists, students or society.

Many have contributed to my interests in defence economics and arms industries, including Todd Sandler, Ron Smith, Paul Dunne, Derek Braddon, David Kirkpatrick, Neil Davies, Keith Hayward, Trevor Taylor, Ron Matthews, Tony Turner, Graham Trevarthen, Ben Solomon, Jacques Fontanel, the late Michael Intriligator and Philip Pugh, among many others. Sophie Ellis, my granddaughter, is my youngest fan and the person who continually asked if the book was finished: she is a hard taskmaster. Special thanks to Steven Gerrard of Agenda Publishing, who first gave me the opportunity to write this book, to two anonymous referees who offered invaluable comments on the original book proposal, and to the referee who read and commented on the final version of the book. I remain responsible for what follows.

The greatest contribution has been from my wife, who for over 50 years has tolerated my obsession with aviation, defence, economics, fly fishing and football. None of my three children have developed an interest in economics, preferring English, human resources and law. This book is dedicated to my grandchildren – Imogen, Sophie, Katie, Matthew and Ollie – they are our hope for the future.

1

THE IMPORTANCE OF ARMS INDUSTRIES

Introduction: the policy issues

Arms producers and arms industries are controversial: they are often criticized and condemned. But such criticisms need to be addressed and carefully considered. Arms firms and whole arms industries cannot be dismissed and proscribed without more detailed and careful analysis and evaluation of their apparent "wrongdoings".

This chapter sets the scene and outlines the policy issues to be explored in the book. Are arms industries important: if so, why, and which other industries are viewed as important? Do they provide "good value for money", or are they inefficient, corrupt and immoral; should they be condemned as "merchants of death"; and do they exploit their market power at the expense of taxpayers? What can and should governments do about them: should privately owned arms firms be subject to tighter government regulation or should they be taken into state ownership, and will state ownership solve the "problem"? These and other questions will be addressed in this book, at the end of which the reader will be able to reach a more informed judgement about the economic aspects of the arms industry. In this chapter, the arguments surrounding the arms industry will be presented and assessed. A legal approach would ask what is the case for the prosecution and what are the arguments for the defence? A starting point requires an explanation of why economists disagree about arms industries and other policy issues, followed by a definition of the arms industry.

Why economists disagree

The typical view of economists is that where there are ten economists there will be ten views and only one will be correct, but no one knows who will be correct!

Economists have good reason to disagree.[1] Their disagreements might focus on differences of view about the relevance of a specific theory (e.g., Keynesians versus monetarists), on whether theories should be accepted or rejected on the basis of their explanatory power and predictive accuracy, or on the realism of their assumptions. Disagreements continue over the accuracy and reliability of evidence and on the appropriateness of particular policy solutions in relation to each economist's value judgements and their views about the best solutions. Here, a distinction arises between positive and normative economics. Positive economics is concerned with *what is* whereas normative economics is about *what ought to be*.

Economists disagree about arms industries for all these reasons. They will disagree about the best economic model for explaining and understanding the behaviour of arms producers, industries and markets. For example, cost overruns and delays on major arms projects are viewed either as the result of firms tackling high-technology problems and uncertainty or as private monopolies exploiting taxpayers. There will also be disagreements about the facts to be explained and the reliability, relevance and acceptability of the evidence. Finally, they will disagree about the best policy solutions, with some preferring market-type solutions (e.g., privatization, or more competition) and others opting for state-type solutions such as state-owned and not-for-profit enterprises. Even definitions of the industry are a source of controversy.

What's in a name? Matters of definition

Arms firms and industries are known by various names. They have been called arms, weapons, military, defence or security industries. Differences of definition often reflect whether the analyst is a peace or defence economist: peace economists prefer the term arms industry whereas defence economists prefer the description defence industry. Care is needed in distinguishing between arms industries and the military, comprising a nation's armed forces in the form of armies, navies and air forces. Armed forces buy arms as inputs into their "production" of defence outputs in the form of peace, protection and security.

Arms industries supply weapons to armed forces both nationally and internationally via exports. They are involved in the design and development (research and development, or R & D), production, servicing and modification of military equipment. They are also involved in training military personnel as well as the management and maintenance of military facilities (e.g., docks, airfields and ranges) together with the disposal of equipment, some of which might involve substantial environmental and "clean-up" costs. For example, disposing of nuclear weapons is costly and time intensive (the process can take up to 50 years). In the case of nuclear-powered submarines, the options include docking at a military shipyard, dumping at sea and temporary safe storage prior to permanent disposal. Russia dumps its nuclear waste at sea (the Kara Sea, north of Siberia); the US uses a nuclear waste repository at Hanford in Washington state; and the UK stores its redundant submarines at Devonport and Rosyth prior to storing its nuclear waste at Capenhurst, Cheshire. Similar disposal and clean-up costs arise for nuclear research and production plants and for storage sites for nuclear weapons.

There are, however, various definitions of arms industries. A narrow definition focuses on *lethal* equipment, comprising lethal air, land and sea equipment. Examples include combat aircraft and helicopters, missiles, tanks and artillery, submarines, aircraft carriers, warships and space systems.[2] Lethal equipment also embraces conventional and nuclear equipment, as well as major projects and small arms (e.g., rifles, ammunition). Indeed, a distinction can be made between the relatively controlled trade in major conventional weapons and the relatively uncontrolled trade in small arms and light weapons. A further dimension embraces the defence electronics industry, which provides the navigation, guidance and communications systems for modern weapons. The emergence of cyber warfare and the companies involved in such activities adds to the challenges of defining arms industries.[3]

There is a broader definition of arms industries that includes all firms supplying goods and services to national defence departments or ministries. Such a definition embraces non-lethal goods and services such as the supply of accommodation, the construction of military bases, the supply of fuel, food and financial services and the supply of motor vehicles, computers and IT systems. The increasing emphasis on the outsourcing of military activities to private contractors has expanded arms markets, allowing new firms to enter markets for activities that were traditionally undertaken "in-house" by the armed forces. Examples include catering, cleaning, transport, training and air tanker operations (e.g., in the UK, RAF air tankers are provided by a private contractor).

There is a further sub-group of weapons: namely, arms firms involved in the supply of weapons of mass destruction (WMD), comprising nuclear, biological and chemical weapons. Biological and chemical weapons are subject to international conventions that outlaw their development, production and stockpiling; but not all nations are signatories to these international conventions and those that are signatories might not abide by the rules. There are also similar international conventions on certain conventional weapons and cluster munitions.

Arms producers are subject to national and international laws that affect their ability to trade, so arms sales that violate such laws form illegal trades. Most large conventional equipment is readily identifiable and is supplied by a small number of large firms, meaning that trade in such equipment is easily regulated and policed by national governments. For example, export sales of aircraft carriers and combat aircraft are difficult to hide and conceal; but export sales of small arms and light weapons (e.g., rifles, ammunition, machine guns, some missiles) are much more easily hidden and can be traded illegally. There are a large number of small firms supplying small arms and this makes their policing more difficult and costly. There is also a demand for illegal arms, with demand coming from non-state groups such as terrorists, rebel groups (freedom fighters) and criminal gangs (e.g., the Mafia). Such demands, often for small arms, can be satisfied by illegal trading, by theft or by acquisition in conflict. Given a demand for illegal trading, arms dealers will emerge to satisfy such demands by bringing together willing sellers and willing buyers. For the purposes of this chapter it is sufficient to recognize that some arms producers supplying small arms and light weapons might be involved in illegal trading (some producers might not be aware of their role in illegal trading: see Chapter 2). Nor are national governments the only buyers of arms; other buyers include private groups and individuals.

New technology affects how we define arms producers and arms industries. For example, manned aircraft only emerged after 1903, leading eventually to today's major aerospace industry, supplying combat aircraft, helicopters, missiles and space systems (including rocket propulsion and moon landings). Aerospace is a completely new industry that did not exist in 1900, and it has resulted in air forces as a new branch of the armed forces. Entry into space has added space to the traditional dimensions of warfare, which now include space weapons and assets (e.g., military satellites). Other examples of technical advance that led to new arms firms include radar, electronics, tanks, nuclear-powered submarines, drones and unmanned air vehicles. More recently, cyber has emerged as a new market, reflecting new threats to national security. Cyber involves markets for software and surveillance technologies that meet an objective that otherwise requires espionage or the use of force. Cyber is an interesting example where the product is not directly lethal but where security is included in one of the definitions of arms industries.

Arms producers and industries are not static: they are changing continuously to meet new threats and new technologies. Some arms firms respond to change by adopting new technologies or by acquiring other firms with relevant technologies and existing markets. Firms that adjust to change successfully will survive; those that fail to adjust will exit the arms industry. For example, BAE Systems has sold many of its civil holdings and acquired a cyber business (BAE 2015). Firms that have exited the aerospace industry include famous aircraft firms (e.g., de Havilland, Hawker, Supermarine and Vickers (all UK); North American and Curtiss–Wright (both US)) and such firms as Swan Hunter (UK) have exited the shipbuilding industry, while other arms firms have exited the industry and entered new civil markets.

Defining and classifying arms producers needs to allow for their defence-dependence (see Table 2.1). Some arms firms supply dual-use products: for example, track can be used for tanks or tractors; steel can be used for warships and bridges; and jet engines are used on both military and civil aircraft. Also, some producers of arms have a high dependence on their arms sales, with such sales accounting for 80 per cent or more of total sales. Questions then arise as to whether firms supplying dual-use products and those with a low defence-dependence are part of the arms industry? One answer is that they qualify as part of the arms industry if they supply their products to a national or foreign defence department or to a national or foreign arms producer.[4] In this case products include goods and services, both lethal and non-lethal, where the supply-side comprises R & D, production, repair, maintenance, modifications and upgrading of equipment. Disposal of arms, especially of WMD, can also be added to the definition of arms industries.

The arms trade is big business and the size of the business varies with war and peace and with international tension (e.g., arms races). The business increases during war, conflict and periods of international tension (e.g., threats, including terrorist threats), all of which lead to increased defence spending. Similarly, business and spending declines with peace and disarmament (e.g., at the end of the First World War, the Second World War and the Cold War), with declining business leading to job losses, plant closures and exits from arms industries. But change is not instantaneous and costless: it takes time and involves adjustment costs (e.g., unemployment, and under-employment of labour and capital resources: see Chapter 9). A further clarification is needed between total defence spending and arms spending. Defence budgets are allocated to acquiring military personnel, arms and other equipment, as well as military facilities (e.g., military bases including airfields, barracks and dockyards). As a result, arms spending forms only part of a nation's total defence budget (e.g., equipment spending might vary from 10 per cent to 30 per cent of a nation's defence budget, where the remaining items of expenditure include personnel, infrastructure and other components).

Arms or defence equipment provides an input into the production of final or overall defence output. The armed forces combine arms with personnel, military facilities (capital such as military bases and communications systems) and other equipment and services to produce overall defence output. However, there is no recognized method of valuing defence output. Traditionally, in many economies, the convention was to assume that inputs equalled outputs (a convention that applied throughout the public sector); but this provided no single valuation of overall defence output. Instead, defence output has been variously described as the provision of peace, protection, deterrence, insurance against future threats and, ultimately, security, but with no single monetary valuation on these outputs. In some economies, defence output is expressed as defence capabilities: for example, the capability to deploy, say, 5,000 combat troops and supporting air and sea forces to the Middle East indefinitely. While this is an improvement over the convention that inputs equal outputs, it lacks a money value for these capabilities: hence, it is not possible to determine whether overall defence spending is a worthwhile investment.

Arms industries are different from the final output of overall defence. For arms, there are market prices comprising input costs and profit margins that reflect the government's and other buyer's willingness to pay. But there are no money valuations that can be placed on the final output of overall defence to provide a single indicator of its value or benefit. In contrast, many civilian goods and services, such as motor cars, televisions and mobile phones, are traded in private competitive markets with large numbers of buyers and sellers determining market prices, showing society's valuation of these products. Defence, however, differs in several key ways from private competitive markets and this explains the challenge in measuring and valuing overall defence output. Nevertheless, all is not lost and economics offers some policy guidelines in this area. The costs of defence and of specific capabilities can be identified and policy-makers can then ask whether defence provides at least a comparable level of benefits. For example, if overall defence spending costs £N billion, does it provide overall benefits of a similar value? The same question can be asked for specific force capabilities, such as nuclear strategic forces, an aircraft carrier capability and a specific combat aircraft capability (e.g., the capability provided by an F-35 combat aircraft).

Different definitions of arms producers and industries affect the size of the industry. A narrow definition based on lethal equipment only would result in a smaller industry than one based on a wider definition that included all sales to national and foreign governments and to national and foreign arms producers. Critics of arms industries need to be clearer about their definitions. Whichever definition is used, the importance of the industry needs to be assessed.

The importance of the industry

Economists assess the economic importance of an industry in terms of its contribution to national output (GDP) compared with the contribution if the resources were used in alternative industries. For example, what is the contribution to GDP of arms industries compared with such alternatives as agriculture, banks and financial services, chemicals, construction, creative industries, electronics, motor vehicles and pharmaceuticals? All industries and services contribute to national output so the key question is which industries maximize national output. In competitive market economies, competition resolves this issue by allocating society's scarce resources between alternative uses so as to maximize national output: hence, an industry in a competitive economy will produce a greater output than its alternatives in other sectors. But real-world economies are not perfectly competitive and private markets often fail to work properly. They might "fail" to work properly because of imperfections such as monopoly power and entry barriers as well as beneficial and harmful externalities (harmful externalities include traffic congestion, noise and pollution: see Tisdell & Hartley (2008)).

Assessing the economic importance of arms industries immediately encounters two major data deficiencies. First, official government statistics on national output do not identify arms industries as a separate and identifiable industrial grouping in any census of production statistics (see Chapter 2).[5] Second, there are no money valuations for the *defence final output* of the arms industry: instead, there are only money values for the *input* costs of arms purchases. Nonetheless, the contribution of arms industries to peace, protection and security for a nation's citizens cannot be ignored: these aspects of defence output have some positive money valuation and society has to reach a judgement on whether the value of these benefits exceeds the cost of supplying arms. One approach is to consider the "Hitler question": namely, what would the UK have been willing to pay to protect itself from invasion by Hitler in 1940? In this context, the UK arms industry supplied the aircraft, tanks and warships that eventually contributed to the defeat of Hitler in 1945 (e.g., Hurricanes, Spitfires, Lancaster, Halifax and Mosquito aircraft). The modern equivalent of the Hitler question would be the possible threats from Russia and IS as well as the general uncertainty about future threats facing all nations. The future is unknown and unknowable, hence the need for some minimum national defence capability to meet such threats. Here, it has to be recognized that defence is not like a water tap that can be turned on and off whenever required. Costs and time are needed to create and train a modern fighting force and these costs can be regarded as an insurance premium to meet unforeseen and unforeseeable contingencies.

In circumstances where there are no money valuations of defence output, assessing the economic importance of arms industries requires alternative measures of importance. These include its economic contribution in terms of employment (jobs) and technology and its contribution to the balance of payments through exports and import-savings (domestic purchases of arms avoids paying for imported arms). But a list of these economic benefits has to be approached critically. First, these benefits need to be compared with the economic benefits that derive from other industries, such as motor vehicles, pharmaceuticals and electronics. This is an empirical question requiring evidence on the economic benefits of alternative industries. Second, in making an economic case for state intervention in arms industries, the economic benefits have to be justified in terms of market failure. Are there failures in labour (jobs), technology (spillovers) and foreign exchange markets (balance of payments)? Next, it is necessary to identify the causes of market failure before identifying appropriate solutions. Typically, a variety of alternative policy solutions are available and it does not follow that arms and arms industries represent the least-cost solution. For example, jobs can be created by construction projects (e.g., building houses, bridges and roads) and more jobs will be created where wage rates are lower than in the arms industry.

Arms, defence and public goods

Arms and arms industries have a further distinctive feature resulting from the public goods nature of defence that represents another source of market failure. Arms and arms industries contribute to defence output. Defence and peace are often presented as classic examples of public goods. These are goods where one person's consumption of defence (or peace) does not affect other people's consumption of defence (non-rivalry), and where once provided, no individual can exclude others from the consumption of defence (non-excludability). For example, the air defence of Moscow is provided to all its citizens: one Moscow citizen's consumption of air defence is not at the expense of any other Moscow citizen, and no Moscow citizen can be excluded from its air defence.

The public goods nature of defence means that left to themselves, private markets will fail to provide the socially desirable amount of defence for a society. As a result, some form of state intervention is needed to correct such market failure and improve the operation of private markets. Once defence is provided, its benefits extend to everyone in society and individuals cannot be excluded from the good by charging a price (cf. the purchase of motor cars). This means that if direct prices cannot be charged, some other method is needed to finance the supply of defence. However, alternative methods of financing defence raise two further problems. First, the "free-rider problem", where a citizen obtains the benefits of defence without contributing to its costs. An example is free riding in NATO, with European member states apparently free riding on US defence spending. Citizens have incentives to conceal their true willingness to pay for defence if its costs will be borne by others in society. Second, if it is difficult to identify each individual citizen's valuation of defence, how does a society or government determine the appropriate or "ideal" size of its defence budget? In democracies, voting systems often have major limitations in allowing voters to express their true preferences for different levels of defence and arms spending (Hartley 2011a: Chapter 4). For example, a general election does not identify each voter's specific preferences for, say, income tax versus social welfare versus education versus foreign policy issues. As a result, elected politicians have discretion in interpreting voter preferences, subject to their desire for re-election. Alternatively, voter preferences on specific issues can be determined more accurately through referendums, but even here, the accuracy and reliability of voter preferences can be affected by the question posed by a referendum and by decisions made by majority voting (compared with alternative voting and decision-making rules). Society needs some mechanism for determining the importance of the arms industries. A legal model or approach to this question would focus on the case for the prosecution and that for the defence.

The legal model: the case for the prosecution

The case against arms industries is varied and extensive, which makes it challenging to distinguish myths, emotion and special pleading from economic and critical analysis and empirical evidence. The task of the economist is to critically evaluate the economic logic of arguments about the arms industry. One could also judge this industry from other perspectives or through different disciplines. For example, educational and medical groups, theologians, religious groups, Quakers, some scientists and peace scientists and other interest groups condemn the industry on ethical and moral grounds (e.g., Campaign Against the Arms Trade (CAAT)). In 2015 Pope Francis condemned arms manufacturers for being "drenched in innocent blood", saying that the arms trade contributed to deaths, injuries and the violation of human rights. Clearly, there are issues of economics versus ethics. Some critics view the arms industry and the military as the "wicked problem" responsible for all the world's ills. The scientific basis of this claim is not addressed. In contrast, this chapter and the book more generally evaluate the arms industry from an *economics* perspective.

Critics claim that arms producers and industries are inefficient monopolies charging high prices and earning monopoly profits at the expense of taxpayers. Furthermore, it is asserted that they supply arms that are not needed, that are characterized by cost overruns, delays in delivery and poor operational performance, and that in some cases have to be cancelled at great cost to the taxpayer and a loss of defence capability for the armed forces. The indictment continues with arms industries accused of starting and promoting wars and conflict and being guilty of bribery and corruption in achieving arms sales, especially arms export sales. These allegations need to be subject to explanation and critical appraisal: a task for which economists are well qualified.[6]

A starting point is ownership and profitability and the need to distinguish between the behaviour of privately owned arms producers and that of state-owned ones. Economic theory establishes a presumption that compared with competitive markets, private monopolies result in higher prices, lower output and abnormal or supernormal profits, leading to a socially undesirable outcome (a misallocation of resources: see Tisdell & Hartley (2008)). In contrast, state-owned monopoly arms producers might act "benevolently" in the "public interest", charging competitive prices and earning only normal profits or zero economic profit.[7] On this basis, critics of arms industries need to distinguish between ownership and profitability, taking care about the definition of profits. State-owned monopoly arms producers might not act benevolently and might be required to act commercially, operating as profit-maximizers, in which case their behaviour will be similar to a private monopoly producer. Also, state-owned enterprises might not be least-cost producers since they are not subject to capital market pressures and, instead, might be subject to "soft budget" constraints (with government-provided funds). Profitability is also confusing since arms producer's reported profits, which are the focus of criticism and condemnation, are typically accounting definitions of profits and not economic definitions of profits.

Critics also claim that arms producers provide arms that are not needed and that are characterized by cost overruns, delays and "gold plating". The assertion that arms industries provide arms that are not needed has to be related to established economic models of defence spending. These suggest that military expenditure, and hence the need for arms, is determined by various factors such as the relative prices of arms and civil goods, a nation's total output (GDP and growth rates), the threats it faces, its membership of military alliances (e.g., NATO), whether it is involved in wars and conflicts, and other variables (e.g., political composition of its government; strategic variables such as the end of the Cold War (Hartley 2011a: Chapter 5)). On this basis, arms are needed to respond to threats, wars and conflict. Weapons are costly and are unlikely to be bought if not needed.

The further claims about costs, delays and gold plating need to be assessed against a standard for comparison. Is a "perfect world" assumed, where there are no cost overruns, no delays and all weapons perform as originally specified? Or, is a real world of uncertainty assumed, where the results of work on high-technology weapons always departs from original plans and where mistakes are made? With uncertainty, no one can accurately predict the future, and today's initial contract estimates for advanced technology weapons will usually be wrong. Arms producers operating at, or beyond, the known frontiers of technology cannot be certain about the unknown and unknowable future. As a result, defence departments have to formulate and award contracts that recognize uncertainty and aim to minimize its costs (see Chapter 7). Threats, technology and governments can change, leading to project cancellations that are often high-profile and widely publicized events. Such cancellations made by governments are not necessarily conclusive evidence of arms producer inefficiency and failure: they might reflect inefficiency and incompetence by the government, or project cancellations might be perfectly sensible and rational government decisions when new technology renders a project obsolescent. Next, evidence is needed on cost escalation and overruns to enable international comparisons of contractual performance. For example, are some nations able to obtain similar types of advanced arms with lower cost overruns, fewer delays and less gold plating? Which are these successful nations and how are such results achieved? Moreover, are other industries and projects also subject to cost overruns, delays, gold plating and project cancellations? Possible examples include major construction projects (e.g., roads, bridges, tunnels) and new developments in motor vehicles, pharmaceuticals or oil exploration. However, private firms rarely publish information on cost overruns, delays or cancellation for their new product developments.

A final set of claims relates to arms producers starting and promoting wars and supporting their activities through bribery and corruption. More specifically, arms exports are alleged to promote regional arms races and contribute to international tension, to waste national resources, to impede economic development and to support oppressive regimes. However, economic models of arms races predict a variety of outcomes. Arms races arise from interdependence between nations' defence spending, reflecting an action–reaction process in which one nation increases its military spending in response to an increase in a potential rival's military spending (e.g., nuclear weapons). Examples of arms races include that during the Cold War between the US and the former Soviet Union, and regional arms races such as those in the Middle East, in India and Pakistan and in North Korea and South Korea. Interestingly, economic models of arms races show that they may contribute to peace through deterrence and that disarmament may be destabilizing, leading to outbreaks of war (Sandler & Hartley 1995: Chapter 4).

Nor is it clear how arms producers start wars. Admittedly, they benefit from the increased defence spending during wars, but if they are so powerful then how do critics explain disarmament and peace, which do not benefit arms producers? Similar condemnation of an industry could be applied to, say, pharmaceutical companies, which might be accused of promoting epidemics, disease and illness, with some products being lethal! Other industries facing similar criticisms and condemnation include motor vehicles, civil nuclear power generation, deep-sea fishing and oil exploration.

Arms producers are also criticized for bribery and corruption, especially in relation to arms exports. Allegations have included arms exports from French, German, British and American arms producers to countries such as Indonesia, Saudi Arabia, South Africa, Tanzania and Venezuela (e.g., BAE Systems in 2010: see Hartley 2012b). Elsewhere, claims have been made of illegal behaviour in relation to arms firms securing domestic contracts (e.g., Boeing in relation to bidding for the US air tanker contract). Problems arise because many of these sales are surrounded in secrecy. Nonetheless, where arms firms are found to be acting illegally, they and their staff should be subject to legal action comprising fines, sanctions and imprisonment.

Bribery and corruption are not confined to arms producers. Other firms outside arms industries have been involved in similar practices, although data are not available to determine whether arms producers are more likely than those in other industries to be involved in bribery and corruption. Examples of other industries involved in corruption include construction, pharmaceuticals (drug companies), gas and oil industries, gas turbines and illegal groups (e.g., Mafia), as well as various sporting activities (e.g., athletics). Corruption distorts markets and leads to unfair competition, and it flourishes where markets function poorly. Defence and security markets represent corruption risks since they involve large contracts that are often shrouded in secrecy and awarded in non-competitive markets. But in principle *all* public sector markets that contract out activities to outside contractors offer opportunities for bribery and corruption as a means of obtaining business.[8]

One further group of arms producers is the focus of special criticism: namely, private military and security companies. Some of these are involved in peaceful activities; others are involved in conflict situations. They provide combat support, including training and intelligence provision, consultancy, security and post-conflict reconstruction. Their security role includes protection tasks such as the guarding of individuals, installations, facilities, pipelines and convoys. Examples include the Constellis Group in the US (previously Academi, formerly Blackwater), Aegis Defence Services and G4S in the UK, the Unity Resources group in Australia, and RSB in Russia. Analysis is complicated by the fact that these companies often change their names! Some of their activities require personnel equipped with small arms, and in a conflict situation (e.g., Iraq) there might be no obvious difference between regular soldiers and private support workers in protecting convoys or installations. Critics demand that private military and security companies should be subject to government regulation forbidding their involvement in direct combat and combat support (Mathieu & Dearden 2006). This raises more general questions about the extent to which military activities can, and should, be allocated to private companies (see Chapter 8).

A further sub-group of private military companies embraces mercenaries and private armies involved in direct combat. Mercenaries are defined as individuals and groups fighting for personal gain rather than national interests (such as in African conflicts like that in the Congo). Criticism focuses on their definition, accountability and legality in lethal combat operations, where the pursuit of personal gain can prolong conflicts and lead to "undesirable" external effects (e.g., civilian casualties). There are international and national laws on mercenaries. The UN Convention on mercenaries has not been signed by all nations, including nations with large military forces (e.g., France, China, India, Russia, the UK and the US). Also, some nations have national laws forbidding their citizens from fighting in foreign wars not involving their nation state (the French Foreign Legion and the British Army's Gurkhas are not classed as mercenaries).

Any study of arms industries cannot ignore the ethical and moral aspects of arms and some types of warfare. Arms industries involve potential clashes between economics, ethics and morality. For example, an economically efficient arms policy might be regarded as unethical and immoral; but, in principle, the contrary might be possible, where economic efficiency might be ethical and moral (there are other combinations for this matrix of economics, ethics and morality, further adding to the controversy surrounding this industry). It could be the case that arms exports were part of an efficient arms policy that might also be viewed as unethical and immoral. Alternatively, ethical and moral policies might create inefficiencies in arms industries. Furthermore, some arms and some forms of warfare might be totally unacceptable, so they are subject to international bans. Examples include chemical and biological weapons, but international bans do not guarantee that all nations will observe the prohibitions. Technical progress might also lead to new weapons that could also be subject to an international ban. For example, the future development of completely autonomous weapons (without human intervention) might be viewed as unethical and immoral.

In summary, the case against arms producers is that they have serious impacts on human rights, security and economic development. Further, it is claimed that the procurement or export of arms might exacerbate conflict, promote aggression or raise tension, support oppressive regimes, undermine democracy and threaten social welfare spending (CAAT 2016a). Not all these claims and assertions have a firm scientific, theoretical and empirical base. Where economics and ethics are in conflict, economists can identify the economic consequences of ethical arms policies, thereby contributing to a more informed debate. Next, the case in favour of arms producers is presented.

The legal model: the case for the defence

Arms industries are justified in terms of their military and economic benefits. They contribute to national security in the form of peace, protection and the security of a nation's citizens, their assets and their national way of life (e.g., freedoms of speech, mobility and culture). These are "goods" that citizens value and for which they are willing to pay. A domestic arms industry contributes to national defence output by providing independence, security of supply and resupply, especially in a conflict. It also provides equipment designed specifically for the nation's armed forces. For example, a domestic arms industry provides arms in a national emergency (e.g., the UK in 1939, with the Hitler question, or in 2017, with threats from IS (Islamic State) and Russia). Arms industries also provide equipment that is needed for international peacekeeping operations, disaster and humanitarian relief missions (e.g., UN operations).

Although such arguments appear impressive, they are not immune from criticism. While citizens value peace and security, their willingness to pay is usually limited (except in national emergencies such as that in the UK in 1939), and the "public goods" and free-rider aspects of defence mean that it is complex to identify a society's true valuation of and willingness to pay for national defence (and international peace and security). Nonetheless, the contribution of a national arms producer to both national and international peace and security has some positive valuation that needs to be incorporated into any economic evaluation of arms producers. However, maintaining a national arms industry to provide independence, security of supply and tailor-made weapons is never cheap and can be costly. Also, specifically designed nationally procured weapons are associated with cost overruns, delays and poor operational performance (see Chapters 7 and 10).

An alternative would be to import arms from foreign producers where their governments have funded all the costs and risks of development and the importing nation pays some contribution to foreign development costs. Compared with nationally procured weapons, imported arms might be cheaper and less risky: their development risks would have been solved with funding from a foreign government. However, a foreign government might cancel the development of a major weapons system, thereby depriving overseas buyers of a required weapon.[9] There are various forms of importing that will reduce some of their risks, especially in relation to independence and security of supply. For example, the importing nation might be willing to manufacture the foreign equipment under licence by creating a domestic final assembly line (e.g., F-16s, F-35s). A foreign buyer might also specify national requirements for equipment, including electronics and engines. For example, in 1966, the UK purchase of US Phantom aircraft required that UK Rolls-Royce engines as well as British avionics be fitted into the aircraft. Similarly, the 1995 UK decision to buy US Apache attack helicopters required local assembly at Yeovil, Somerset, with Rolls-Royce engines and UK electronics. Admittedly, licensed production and design modifications are not costless but they might be cheaper than the national development and small-scale production of domestically produced weapons. This becomes an empirical question requiring evidence on the total development costs and the unit production costs of independence compared with direct imports and licensed production with or without modifications. An alternative policy solution to independence and security of supply might be provided by membership of a military alliance (e.g., NATO).

National arms producers provide additional economic benefits in the form of employment, technology and spillovers, and a contribution to the balance of payments. Some of these arguments were assessed above in examining the importance of the industry. The employment benefits of arms industries are claimed to include the total numbers of jobs, their skill and wage levels and their location. Supporters of arms industries point to "large" numbers of jobs dependent on major weapons programmes (e.g., F-35s and the UK

Trident replacement) and the fact that many of these jobs are highly skilled and highly paid, and therefore improve living standards. Some of these jobs, especially in the supply chain, might be located in remote areas where there are few alternative job opportunities. The problem with arguments about employment benefits is that all economic activity generates and supports jobs. The jobs argument is inevitably deployed to justify any new activity, such as fracking or mining and quarrying in scenic and environmentally protected areas. The question then becomes one of evidence on magnitudes. Which activities support the greatest number of jobs per unit of expenditure and what are their wage levels (more jobs will be created at lower wage levels)? Arms producers also provide substantial numbers of highly paid jobs (e.g., compared with large numbers of low-paid jobs in fast food outlets). But other industries also provide high-skilled and highly paid jobs, including chemicals, electronics, financial services and pharmaceuticals.

Market failure in labour markets also has to be considered. Often, labour markets work well as clearing mechanisms, although some local failures are reflected in relatively high regional unemployment rates. Even where labour markets fail to work properly, it does not follow that arms projects are the only or least-cost solution to maintaining employment. Other policies such as training and retraining, information, mobility allowances, vocational guidance and assistance with job search also contribute to assisting labour to find other jobs elsewhere in the economy.

Some critics of arms industries assert that the industry is in long-term decline and that it receives massive state financial subsidies that could be better used to support renewable energy industries (e.g., offshore wind and marine energy). Their claim is that renewable energy would provide more jobs than arms industries, it would provide alternative employment for arms industry workers, the jobs would be high skilled and there would be thousands of supply chain jobs that could be located anywhere in the country. It is also claimed that investment in renewable energy would place nations such as the UK in a leading position in technologies that will be in high demand, with major export potential (CAAT 2016b). However, just as critics of arms industries make their case against the industry, their arguments about alternative resource uses also need to be critically assessed and evaluated. Proposals to reallocate resources from arms industries to renewable energy take a simple view of resource reallocation that is, in reality, costly, complex and takes time. Privately owned and profit-seeking firms and markets are central to resource allocation. It cannot be assumed that arms producers that have a competitive advantage in arms markets will automatically reallocate their business to renewable energy markets: these are new emerging and risky markets and arms producers and their workforces might prefer other industries. Uncertainty is a further factor in resource choices. While renewable energy currently has superficial attractions, in a world of uncertainty today's winners might be tomorrow's losers; it is also the case that firms other than arms producers might be better able to exploit new energy markets (see Chapter 9).

Arms industries provide further economic benefits in the form of technology and spin-offs. There are some attractive examples of spin-offs from arms industries, including radar, jet engines, the Internet, composite materials, space communications, drones and helicopter rotor blades (e.g., applied to wind farms). But attractive though these examples are, they do not provide any indication of the *market value* of spin-offs: how worthwhile are they? Also, some technologies might be defence specific: only of value in the arms industry (e.g., stealth technology). Other industries might also provide valuable spin-offs. There is a more fundamental issue, relating to whether R & D markets fail to work properly, therefore requiring state intervention to improve their operation. In relation to technology spin-offs, R & D markets might fail to work properly if it is too costly to establish property rights in valuable ideas and knowledge. Again, however, it does not follow that arms projects are the most effective or least-cost method of correcting failures in R & D markets.

Defence industries provide further economic benefits through arms exports, which contribute to the balance of payments, provide jobs and maintain industrial capacity. For example, it is argued that export sales contribute to retaining defence industrial capacity, and without such sales national governments would have to bear the costs of retaining capacity. Assessing the retention-of-capacity argument assumes that such capacity is needed in the future and fails to recognize that there might be alternative solutions, such as importing or "mothballing" capacity, each of which involves different costs.

There is a further contribution to the balance of payments in the form of import-savings. Buying arms from a national industry "saves" on the foreign currency required for alternative imports. But estimating the magnitude of such savings requires that domestic purchases be valued on the basis of the least-cost alternative, where imports might be considerably cheaper than a domestic buy (assuming that imports are close substitutes for a domestic weapon). And both the arms export and import-saving contributions to the balance of payments have to be related to major market failures in foreign currency markets. Typically, such markets work very well and are unlikely to be characterized by market failure.

One study of the economic costs and benefits of a 50 per cent reduction in UK defence exports estimated that the economic costs were relatively small and mostly one-off. It concluded that the balance of arguments about defence exports should largely revolve around non-economic considerations. The study had its limitations: it was not a comprehensive cost–benefit analysis of UK defence exports and it applied a specific economic model with time lags and used the standard economic assumption that everything else in the economy remains unchanged (Chalmers *et al.* 2002).

There is a more fundamental concern about the economic benefits of arms industries. The focus on jobs, spillovers and exports diverts attention from the real aims of defence policy: to provide peace, protection and security to a nation's citizens. Arms purchases that contribute to national defence are not designed to protect a nation's jobs, technology and exports.

Conclusion

This chapter has reviewed the economic aspects of arguments for and against the arms industry. It has shown that the issues are complex, with varying interpretations. At the most basic, there are problems in defining an arms industry and assessing its economic importance. Next, many of the arguments about the industry lack reliable and reputable data to reach a conclusion. As always, there are no answers except to questions, and no views except from a viewpoint. Economists have the task of identifying and critically assessing the economic questions about arms industries.

Arms industries are not costless. Some of their costs are reflected in government defence budgets. Also, where there is conflict, there are further costs reflected in the deaths and destruction caused by war. Evidence of military deaths are readily available in British cathedral and church grave-yards, where there are memorials to military personnel killed in colonial wars, the two Great Wars and conflicts since 1945 (the price of empire?). For the Soviet Union, the total number of deaths in the Second World War has been estimated at over 20 million military and civilian personnel. But success in conflict has its benefits. For example, the Allied defeat of Nazi Germany in the Second World War resulted in the end of slavery, the res-toration of freedom, liberty and peace for the citizens of occupied Western Europe. But none of this confirms that arms industries are solely responsible for wars, their costs and consequences. A whole range of factors account for war and peace. Our next task is to review the facts about the arms industry.

Notes

1. Churchill is reputed to have said that if you put two economists in a room, you get two opinions, unless one of them is Lord Keynes, in which case you will get three opinions, since Keynes will say: on the one hand and on the other. The author is similarly guilty of frequent use of "on the one hand ... and on the other". This book comes with the usual health warnings about economists.
2. The UN Outer Space Treaty (1967) prohibits weapons of mass destruction in space but it does not prohibit conventional weapons being placed in space.
3. Cyber warfare is Internet-based conflict. It involves attacks on computers and information networks (e.g., computer viruses), and armed forces are highly dependent on information systems (e.g., for knowledge and communications).
4. An example would be BAE Systems supplying Typhoons to the Saudi Arabian government and Martin Baker (UK) supplying ejector seats to Boeing for its F-18E/F Super Hornets for sale to the US Navy or for export to other nations. Care is needed to avoid double counting.
5. The UK census of production only identifies two defence-specific industries, namely, the manufacture of weapons and ammunition (Standard Industrial Classification (SIC) 25.4) and the manufacture of fighting vehicles (SIC 30.4). Other major arms sectors such as aerospace and shipbuilding are only identified for their total output, comprising both military and civil output: the defence sales of these industries are not shown separately.
6. Critics refer to the role and performance of economists in the Brexit debate, which showed the limitations of their qualifications in that debate.
7. Economists distinguish between normal and abnormal or supernormal profits. Normal profits are those that are sufficient to persuade firms to remain in the industry and represents the opportunity cost of capital. Abnormal or super-normal profits are profits that are greater than normal and are associated with temporary shortages or monopoly power. Supernormal profits are economic

or pure profits that are earnings in excess of all opportunity costs of capital. Accounting profits differ from economic profits: accounting definitions of costs exclude the opportunity cost of capital and a risk premium. To economists, the opportunity cost of capital is a cost, whereas accountants include it as part of profits (Lipsey & Chrystal 1995: 187–8).

8. Transparency International publishes a Corruption Perception Index. In 2015 it showed that 68 per cent of the world's nations had a serious corruption problem. Also, from a total of 168 countries in 2015, Denmark ranked top of the index (low corruption), with Germany and the UK ranked at tenth and the USA ranked at sixteenth. At the other end of the ranking were Afghanistan (ranked at 166) and North Korea and Somalia (each ranked at 167, indicating high levels of corruption). Further opportunities for corruption arise from transactions between private firms (i.e. firm to firm transactions), where corruption and bribery are even more difficult to identify (TI 2015).

9. An example occurred in 2017 when there were reports that President Donald Trump threatened to cancel the US F-35B aircraft, which would leave the UK without an aircraft for its new aircraft carriers. In such an eventuality, the UK could continue to fund development costs for the F-35.

2

THE FACTS

Introduction: the issues

What are the facts about the world's arms industries? What is known, what is not known and what do we need to know for making sensible policy choices about arms industries? We need to know which countries are the world's major arms spenders and which are the major arms companies and industries, we need to know their size measured by annual sales and employment, and we need to know where they are located. Information is also needed on arms R & D spending, arms exports and the trade in small arms.

What is known?

There is only a limited literature on the economics of the world's arms industries, much of it dated. A classic pioneering book dealt with *The Economics of Defense in the Nuclear Age* (Hitch & McKean 1960) and this was followed by *The Weapons Acquisition Process: An Economic Analysis* (Peck & Scherer 1962).[1] Subsequent publications have included *NATO Arms Co-operation* (Hartley 1983) and *The Political Economy of Aerospace Industries* (Hartley 2014).

Statistical data provides an alternative method for dealing with what is known about the world's arms industries. For a sector dominated by security concerns, there is a surprising variety of published sources.

Examples include the Stockholm International Peace Research Institute, with its yearbooks and databases (SIPRI 2016a,b,c) providing data on military expenditure, arms transfers and the world's top 100 arms companies. Reports from the World Military Expenditures and Arms Transfers provide data on military expenditure, armed forces personnel and arms transfers (WMEAT 2016). Further sources include the Small Arms Survey (SAS 2015), the annual volumes called *The Military Balance* that are produced by the International Institute for Strategic Studies (IISS 2016), and various reports from the US Congressional Research Service (CRS: Washington, DC) and the Rand Corporation (Santa Monica, CA). Other data sources include national defence ministries, company annual reports and industry trade associations.

A nation's total military spending is a starting point in identifying the major arms spending nations. Total military spending comprises more than arms spending: it includes spending on military personnel, bases and facilities. Typically, arms spending accounts for some 15 per cent of total defence spending, but higher-spending nations are more likely to be capital intensive, with higher shares of arms spending.[2] Of course, not all arms expenditure is spent within a nation. Nonetheless, the data in Table 2.1 provide a starting point in identifying the world's leading arms spending nations, with the US dominating the list.

Much more is known about arms firms and industries. The world's major prime contractors are well known, including firms such as Airbus, BAE Systems, Boeing, Lockheed Martin and Northrop Grumman. US companies dominate the world arms market, as shown in Table 2.2. In 2015, they accounted for seven of the top ten and 55 per cent of the top 20 arms companies in the world. Within that top 20, the average US firm is some 35 per cent larger than its European rivals in terms of annual sales, with higher US labour productivity. If the average European arms firm achieved US scales of output and productivity levels, there would be a reduction in the number of major European firms in the world top 20 from six to around four. Such potential reductions suggest excess capacity in Europe, where there are too many relatively small firms. Table 2.2 also shows that the major Russian arms firms are at a competitive disadvantage within the top 20 firms: they are massively labour intensive with low labour productivity.

Table 2.1 Major military spending nations, 2015

Country	Total military spending (US$m)	Country	Total military spending (US$m)
USA	596,024	Italy	23,840
China	214,787	Australia	23,588
Saudi Arabia	87,186	Israel	16,101
Russia	66,421	Turkey	15,275
UK	55,460	Canada	15,031
India	51,257	Spain	14,104
France	50,860	Poland	10,460
Japan	40,885	Algeria	10,413
Germany	39,393	Iran	10,265
South Korea	36,435	Colombia	9,871
Brazil	24,584	Pakistan	9,510

Notes. An arbitrary cut-off point was selected at $9,500m so the list of nations is not comprehensive. For smaller-spending nations the list is illustrative rather than comprehensive. Figures are in current 2015 prices.
Source: SIPRI (2015).

Table 2.2 also shows each firm's dependence on arms sales. There are considerable variations in arms sales dependency, reflecting different firm views on their preferred "mix" of arms and civil sales and their preferred solution to achieving profitability. The extremes are firms such as Bechtel and Airbus at the low arms dependency end (14–18%) and firms like BAE Systems, Raytheon and Huntington Ingalls that have relatively high arms dependency (93–96%). Some of the largest arms firms are characterized by their relatively high dependence on military sales. Firms with a high arms dependency are more likely to encounter "adjustment problems" when shifting from military to civil markets (see Chapter 9).

The US and UK firms in the top 20 are all privately owned, while elsewhere, some of the French, Italian and Russian arms firms in the top 20 are either state owned or partly state owned. Aerospace firms – working on aircraft, missiles, space systems and electronics – dominate the top ten: no specialist land and sea systems firms appeared in the top 10 list for 2015. Three business models feature in the top 20 firms. First, defence specialists

Table 2.2 Top 20 arms companies, 2015

Company	Country	Arms sales (US$m)	Arms employment	Arms dependency (%)
Lockheed Martin	USA	36,440	99,540	79
Boeing	USA	27,960	46,806	29
BAE Systems	UK	25,510	76,725	93
Raytheon	USA	21,780	57,340	94
Northrop Grumman	USA	20,060	55,900	86
General Dynamics	USA	19,240	60,939	61
Airbus	Europe	12,860	24,583	18
United Technologies	USA	9,500	31,552	16
Finmeccanica (renamed Leonardo)	Italy	9,300	30,654	65
L-3 Communications	USA	8,770	31,920	84
Thales	France	8,100	32,339	52
Huntington Ingalls	USA	6,740	34,080	96
Almaz-Antey	Russia	6,620	94,176	95
Safran	France	5,020	18,223	26
Harris Corp	USA	4,920	13,860	66
Rolls-Royce	UK	4,790	11,615	23
United Aircraft Corp	Russia	4,610	80,000	80
Bechtel Corp	USA	4,600	7,420	14
United Shipbuilding Corp	Russia	4,510	235,340	87
Booz Allen Hamilton	USA	3,900	16,272	72
Average: USA		14,901	41,421	72
Average: Europe		10,930	32,349	39
Average: n = 17		13,499	38,219	66

Notes. (i) Companies are the top 20 firms from the top 100 arms producers and military service companies in the world, excluding China. Companies are ranked by arms sales in 2015 prices. (ii) Arms employment as estimated by the author by applying arms sales shares in total sales to total company employment assuming that labour productivity is identical between military and civilian markets (a heroic assumption!). Arms employment for Russian firms based on 2014 data. (iii) Arms dependency is arms share of total company sales. (iv) Averages. China is not included in the SIPRI Top 100. Subsidiaries are excluded. Average for Europe based on six companies (excluding Russian companies); aggregate average is for 17 companies from USA (n = 11) and Europe (n = 6), excluding Russia. Average arms dependency is based on the median figure.

Source: SIPRI (2016a).

involved in a range of air, land and sea systems and defence electronics (e.g., Lockheed Martin, BAE Systems). Second, specialist aerospace firms specializing in military and civil aircraft, aero-engines and other aerospace systems (Airbus, Boeing, Rolls-Royce, Safran). Third, diversified firms supplying a varied range of arms and civil markets, including IT, management consultancy, construction and civil engineering (Betchel, Harris, Booz Allen Hamilton). Among the top US firms, Huntington Ingalls is different since it is a major shipbuilder, supplying warships and nuclear-powered submarines; it was a spin-off from Northrop Grumman (2011) and includes Newport News Shipbuilding. More detailed analysis of the top 5 firms shows that they have a high defence dependency (median of 86%). Boeing is an exception as it has a high dependency on its civil airliner business.

There are other major arms companies and countries in the world top 100 and some examples are shown in Table 2.3. Unsurprisingly, the average size of firms in this group is considerably smaller than the average in the top 20, and some companies are extremely labour intensive with low labour productivity. Table 2.3 also shows the extensive geographical distribution of the world's arms firms, with firms located in Australia, Brazil, India, Israel, Singapore and South Korea. Also, firms below the top 20 contained specialist land and sea systems producers (not shown in Table 2.3). Examples include Indian Ordnance Factories, Nexter in France (formerly GIAT, specializing in land systems) and Krauss-Maffei Wegman in Germany (Leopard tanks; in 2015, KMW created a joint company with Nexter).

Some arms companies publish useful quantitative and qualitative information in their annual company reports. However, companies often conduct a range of military and civil business and only report on their *total* sales, employment and profitability: they do not separately identify their arms activities. There are exceptions, though: BAE Systems, for example, provides detailed sales, profitability and employment data for each of its defence divisions. An example is presented in Table 2.4, where comparisons can be made between the productivity and profitability of each of BAE's divisions in 2015 (BAE 2015). Its US platforms business reported low profitability compared with the overall performance of the company, and the cyber division's productivity and profitability were below the company average. It is also worth noting BAE's divisional structure, comprising electronics, cyber, and platforms and services in the US, UK and International divisions. Other arms companies have different divisional structures that reflect the composition of their businesses and their varied efforts to minimize transaction costs. For example, in 2014, Lockheed Martin had five divisions – aeronautics, information systems, missiles, space systems, and mission systems and training – while Northrop Grumman had four: aerospace, electronics, information systems and technical services.

Table 2.3   Other arms companies in the rest of the world, 2015.

Rank	Company	Country	Arms sales (US$m)	Arms employment	Arms dependency (%)
28	Mitsubishi Heavy Industries	Japan	2,970	7,030	9
29	Elbit Systems	Israel	2,950	11,524	95
30	Rheinmetall	Germany	2,870	10,340	50
33	Saab	Sweden	2,640	12,046	82
36	Hindustan Aeronautics	India	2,340	29,540	91
52	LIGNex1	S Korea	1,680	3,150	100
53	ST Engineering	Singapore	1,660	8,060	36
60	Polish Armaments Group	Poland	1,190	16,200	90
69	ASELSAN	Turkey	1,000	4,821	97
72	Austal	Australia	980	1,158	97
79	Pilatus Aircraft	Switzerland	870	1,433	75
81	UkrOboronProm	Ukraine	870	76,000	95
88	Embraer	Brazil	810	3,169	14
92	CAE	Canada	760	3,120	39
93	Kongsberg Group	Norway	730	2,692	35
	Average (n = 15)		1,621	12,686	82

Notes. (i) This table shows examples of other arms companies from the rest of the world. Other companies were selected on the basis of their being the largest firm in a nation not listed in the top 20 (Table 2.2). Only one company was reported for each nation and the results are meant to be illustrative only. (ii) Subsidiaries not included. Average arms dependency is based on the median figure.

Source: SIPRI (2016a).

Table 2.4   BAE Systems, 2015.

Division	Sales (£m)	Profitability (% return on sales)	Employment	Labour productivity (£000s)
Electronic Systems	2,638	15.0	12,400	212,742
Cyber & Intelligence	1,848	7.8	12,900	143,256
Platforms & Services (US)	2,779	6.4	11,500	241,652
Platforms & Services (UK)	7,405	9.7	29,600	250,169
Platforms & Services (International)	3,742	9.0	13,600	275,147
BAE total	17,904	9.4	82,500	217,018

Note. Labour productivity calculated from sales and employment data. HQ included in "BAE total" figures.

Source: BAE (2015).

While nations other than the US are represented in the world top 100, US firms continue to dominate. Table 2.5 shows the geographical distribution of the world's top 100 arms companies. In 2015, US and European arms firms accounted for 65 per cent of the top 100 firms, followed by Russia, South Korea, India, Israel and Japan. Within Europe, the UK and France were dominant, accounting for some 50 per cent of the top European arms firms. However, such data do not show the regional and local distributions of arms producers within each country (e.g., some towns are one-company towns dependent on arms producers).

Supply chains

A focus on prime contractors gives only a limited view of the arms industry. Each prime contractor has a network of suppliers providing inputs for the manufacture of its final product. For example, for the manufacture of combat aircraft, specialist firms supply engines, ejector seats, radar, computer equipment and landing gear. These are first-tier suppliers, and there are further firms at the second, third and fourth tiers of the supply chain. Indeed, supply chains are complex and extensive and can be compared with an iceberg: the prime contractor represents the tip of the iceberg, acting as final assembler of major weapons projects.

Table 2.5   World distribution of major arms firms, 2015.

Country	Number of arms firms in top 100
USA	38
Europe:	27
UK	9
France	6
Russia	10
South Korea	7
India	3
Israel	3
Japan	3
Switzerland	2
Turkey	2
Australia	1
Brazil	1
Poland	1
Singapore	1
Ukraine	1

Note. Based on number of arms firms in SIPRI Top 100 arms firms in the world, excluding China. European total includes UK and France. All ranked by annual arms sales.
Source: SIPRI (2016a).

Recognition of supply chains makes it difficult to identify the true extent of a nation's defence industry, and this forms one of the unknowns about arms industries. A study of the supply chain for the UK Warrior armoured fighting vehicle identified some 200 first-level suppliers located in various parts of Britain, all supplying the prime contractor located at Telford, near Shrewsbury. In turn, first-level suppliers used an average of 18 suppliers, second-level firms had an average of 7 suppliers, and third-tier firms had an average of 2–3 suppliers (Hartley *et al.* 1997). In some cases, second- and third-tier suppliers did not know that they were involved in defence work. Examples include steel stockholders and distributors and suppliers of ball bearings (which can be used in tanks or tractors).

Supply chains are important for policy-makers since governments often focus solely on the primes when considering the consequences of their actions. For example, a decision to cancel a major weapons project will affect the prime contractor and the firms in its supply chain, some of which might be highly dependent on defence business and might be major employers in a town or the only employer in a remote rural area.

Measuring the size of arms industries

Size is measured by sales and employment both currently and over time to identify trends. New technology has led to the emergence of new firms and industries. For example, in 1900, air forces and the aircraft industry did not exist, nor did today's major arms firms such as Airbus, Boeing, BAE Systems and Lockheed Martin. Similarly, in 1900, the jet engine had not been invented nor had precision guided missiles, helicopters, unmanned air vehicles (UAVs), radar, electronics or space and nuclear systems.

These new technologies revolutionized arms markets, leading to new firms and new industries. Examples included the emergence of the jet engine and nuclear propulsion industries (e.g., General Electric, Pratt and Whitney, Rolls-Royce and Safran (Snecma)), helicopters (e.g., Airbus Helicopters, Leonardo Helicopters, Sikorsky) and the defence electronics industry (e.g., L-3, ITT, Honeywell, Ultra Electronics). Electronics formed major parts of missiles and intercontinental ballistic missiles (ICBMs) with nuclear warheads, further revolutionizing warfare after 1944 (starting with the German V-1 and V-2 weapons in 1944). The new technologies had major substitution effects on the armed forces. Nuclear weapons replaced large-scale conventional forces, missiles replaced artillery, and close support aircraft and helicopters replaced tanks. New technology also required R & D inputs, leading arms firms to become R & D-intensive firms. Recently, arms companies have entered new markets for UAVs and for cyber, intelligence, information and security systems (e.g., responding to terrorist threats). In some cases, arms firms have changed their names. Examples include Leonardo (formerly Finmeccanica, Italy), BAE Systems (formerly British Aerospace, UK) and Thales (formerly Thomson-CSF, France).

While considerable information is available on the world's major arms *firms*, much less is known about the size of national defence *industries*. Data on current industry sales and employment and time trends are difficult to obtain. National governments often do not provide official statistics on their defence industries, usually because of the difficulties of defining them. At best, official government industry census data will show statistics for industries such as aerospace and shipbuilding, both of which have a mix of military and civil business and are regarded as defence-dependent industries. For example, the UK Ministry of Defence (MoD) used to publish annual statistics on national and regional employment dependent on UK defence spending and defence exports. But in 2009 it decided to discontinue publishing such statistics, saying that the "data do not directly support MoD policy-making and operations". Also, it was stated that the UK defence budget was never allocated on a regional basis, nor were decisions about where contracts with industry were placed taken to benefit one region or industry over another (MoD 2009: Chapter 1). Concern was also expressed about the accuracy of some of the employment figures.

As an alternative to the absence of official statistics, limited data are sometimes provided by the national industry trade association. Inevitably, industry trade associations use different definitions of their defence industries, leading to different coverage (e.g., some include aerospace; some exclude security and cyber firms); trade association members include specialist arms companies as well as firms supplying both arms and civil markets; and there might be different measures of employment comprising direct and indirect numbers. For some countries, it is almost impossible to obtain any data on the size of their national defence industries (e.g., North Korea and some African nations). Table 2.6 provides some limited data on the size of national defence industries measured by employment. The numbers were mostly obtained from national defence industry trade associations and should be treated as indicative of the general orders of magnitude. Predictably, given the size of their national military budgets, the US, Russia, China and European countries dominate the list of major arms employers. However, employment numbers are not an indicator of industrial efficiency: labour is only one input into arms production, and efficiency requires that inputs be related to outputs (e.g., via productivity measures).

Table 2.6 Employment in arms industries.

Industry	Employment (000s)	Industry	Employment (000s)
USA	800–3,500	Russia	2,000
Canada	109	China	953
UK	277	India	338
France	400	Israel	50
Germany	90	Turkey	41
Italy	47	Pakistan	40
Sweden	20	Iran	35+
Spain	18	Australia	27
Netherlands	12	Brazil	25
Finland	7	Japan	24
Norway	5	Singapore	23
Total Europe	442	South Africa	15

Notes: (i) Data are for various dates, mostly for 2012–14. Some are earlier but were the latest available at the time of this study (e.g., China (2005), Iran (2007), Spain (2010), India (2011)). (ii) Some are the author's estimates (e.g., Europe, where totals included aerospace employment and the author excluded civil aerospace employment from the total). Also, Europe is defined as 17 EU nations plus Norway, Switzerland and Turkey. (iii) Most employment totals are for direct employment, excluding indirects, which represent employment in the supply chain. Also, induced employment is excluded except for USA where the higher figure comprises direct, indirect and induced employment and includes aerospace employment. Direct employment is often defined as employment in the firms providing goods or services directly to the national defence department or ministry. (iv) For Japan and Singapore, employment totals were based on employment in major arms companies and hence are lower-bound estimates. Singapore was represented by Singapore Technology Engineering and Japan by Mitsubishi, Kawasaki and NEC.

Sources: AeroSpace and Defence Industries Association of Europe (2014), Behera (2013), Dorman *et al.* (2015).

Defence R & D

Issues of secrecy also mean that defence R & D spending and the numbers of scientists and technologists employed in arms firms and industries are often veiled in mystery. All governments hide details of their new arms programmes (e.g., "black" programmes in the US), especially when it comes to developments in nuclear weapons research (e.g., Iran, Israel and North Korea). Nonetheless, there are published data on defence R & D spending by nation. Table 2.7 shows defence R & D spending by the US, major European countries and other nations in 2014. Four points can be stressed. First, US defence R & D spending greatly exceeds the aggregate total for the EU and for other nations, providing the US arms industry with a comparative technological advantage. Second, comparisons with the EU total are misleading since the EU comprises separate individual states and is not a single state entity. Third, the UK, France and Germany account for 93 per cent of total EU defence R & D spending. Fourth, substantial defence R & D spending as seen in Australia, Canada, Japan, Korea and Turkey suggests the development of national arms industries in those countries, leading to the creation of new entrants to the arms market. Data are not available for China, Israel or North Korea.

Arms exports

There is substantial international trade in arms. Weapons producers sell their products to national and foreign governments as well as to national and foreign firms (e.g., aero-engines and avionics are supplied to aircraft firms). Data are available on the world's arms exports. Table 2.8 shows world arms deliveries and the top seven arms suppliers in 2014, including their share of sales to developing nations. The US dominates the list, accounting for 26 per cent of world arms deliveries in 2014, followed by Russia and France. China's arms exports are wholly to developing nations. Typically, arms exports comprise air and land systems. Care is needed in interpreting and analysing arms export data. Different definitions are used, embracing value and volume data for deliveries or orders or payments, with some definitions confined to arms alone and others including spares, support and training. On this basis, arms export figures might not be directly comparable. Offsets are a further complication, where the exporter offers some work share to the importing country (e.g., licensed production of final assembly). As a result, not all of the total value of exports represents an injection of spending power into the exporting nation (see Chapter 7).

Table 2.7 Defence R & D spending, 2014.

Country	US$m
Europe	
UK	2,459.5
France	1,199.2
Germany	947.4
Poland	198.3
Sweden	140.0
Spain	112.7
Italy	90.3
Netherlands	71.8
Finland	45.5
Czech Republic	18.4
Total EU	**9,845.7**
Rest of world	
USA	69,713.4
Russia	1,794.5
Korea	2,721.5
Japan	1,534.2
Turkey	656.2
Australia	297.9
Canada	246.2
Taiwan	191.3

Notes. (i) R & D spending is for government-funded defence R & D. Russian data are for 2000: no recent data available; Canada for 2013. (ii) Data from EDA (2016) and OECD (2016).
Sources: EDA (2016), OECD (2016).

Small arms

A further sector of the arms industry is identified separately: namely, the trade in small arms and light weapons. These include ammunition, revolvers, rifles, machine guns, mortars and portable launchers of anti-aircraft missiles. Information on this sub-sector is provided annually by the Small

Arms Survey. An early estimate suggested that employment in small arms firms in Russia totalled almost 80,000 personnel in 2001, while the corresponding figure for US small arms producers was 17,000. In 2001 at the global level there were 1,134 companies producing small arms in 30 countries (Small Arms Survey 2003). The actors involved in this market included private security companies as well as those involved in the illicit craft production of arms. In fact, illegal trading is a feature of the small arms market, with small arms supplied to non-state armed, terrorist and rebel groups (e.g., IS, al Qaeda and other jihadists).

Table 2.8 World arms deliveries, 2014.

Nation	Deliveries (US$m, 2014 prices)	Percentage to developing nations
USA	12,180	63
Russia	9,200	91
France	5,100	49
UK	3,000	53
China	1,800	100
Germany	1,800	61
Italy	1,200	42
Total	46,780	44

Notes. (i) Data are for deliveries. There are other data for worldwide agreements that show orders where orders can be distributed over a number of years. Arms exports comprise all types of weapons, spares, military assistance, construction and training. (ii) Percentage for developing nations shows, for each exporter, its share of sales to developing nations: for example, China's arms exports are 100 per cent to developing nations.
Source: Theohary (2015).

Information is available on the main exporters of small arms. These include established major arms industries as well as some that are less well known, such as Austria, Bulgaria, Mexico, the Philippines, Serbia and Taiwan (see Table 2.9). The fact that some of the world's major exporters of conventional weapons have a low ranking for small arms suggests that these nations do not have a competitive advantage in small arms and light weapons (e.g., France and the UK). Over the period 2001–12, the nations that experienced the largest increase in their small arms exports, suggesting a comparative advantage in the market, were China (1,456%), Norway (777%), South Korea (636%), Turkey (467%), Brazil (295%), Russia (273%) and Israel (256%) (SAS 2015).

Table 2.9 Small arms exporters, 2012.

Export Value (US$)	Exporters (listed in descending order of value of exports)
$500 million or more	USA, Italy
$100-$499 million	Germany, Brazil, Austria, S. Korea, Russia, China, Belgium, Czech, Turkey, Norway, Japan
$50-$99 million	UK, Spain, Israel, Croatia, Finland, Canada, Switzerland, Mexico, France, Serbia
$10-$49 million	Sweden, India, Philippines, Singapore, Portugal, Hungary, Bulgaria, Argentina, Taiwan, Cyprus, Romania, Australia, Ukraine, Denmark, Poland

Note. North Korea is a major exporter of small arms but data on its arms exports are not available.
Source: SAS (2015).

Some of the major small arms firms are ATK (ammunition, USA), Beretta (Italy), Chemring (UK), CBC (ammunition, Brazil), FN Herstal (Belgium), Heckler and Koch (Germany), Igman (ammunition, Bosnia), Glock (pistols, Austria), Indian and Pakistan Ordnance Factories, IWI (Israel), Nexter (France), RUAG (ammunition, Switzerland), Smith and Wesson (US), Sellier and Bellot (ammunition, Czech Republic: a subsidiary of CBC) and Zastava (Serbia). Many small arms companies are dual use, also supplying firearms for civilian markets (personal defence and sporting uses).

Regulation of arms exports

International trade in arms is subject to regulation through the UN Arms Trade Treaty (2014), which regulates the international trade in conventional arms including small arms and obliges member states to comply with arms embargoes. There is also a UN Programme of Action that promotes voluntary cooperation to prevent and eradicate illicit trade in small arms and light weapons, but it is not a UN Treaty and critics claim that it has not been effective. Further regulation is imposed by some nation states. For example, the US Arms Control Act (1976) regulates the import and export of arms and defence services and allows arms exports for legitimate self-defence. The UK has a parliamentary committee on arms export controls that provides regular reports on UK arms exports and its arms exports policy. For example, in 2016 it issued a report on the use of UK-manufactured weapons supplied to Saudi Arabia and their possible use in the Yemen conflict (House of Commons 2016).

New entrants

New entry into the *major* weapons systems market is difficult and costly (e.g., nuclear weapons, combat aircraft, missiles, nuclear-powered submarines, warships). Entry barriers mean that new entrants have to compete with a group of established firms with demonstrated technological and price competitive advantages (e.g., BAE Systems, Lockheed Martin). Established arms firms for major weapons systems have the advantage of government support from funding and procurement. Nonetheless, new entrants are always emerging. Examples include new firms from Brazil, China, India, Israel, Japan, Pakistan, South Africa, South Korea and Turkey. Further new suppliers are emerging from Central and Eastern Europe (Bulgaria, Czech Republic, Hungary, Poland). Firms include the Paramount Group in South Africa (light attack aircraft), Hyundai Rotem in South Korea (military vehicles) and the WBE group in Poland (defence electronics). Such new entrants might receive government support, they might have identified a new market opportunity, they might have a local competitive advantage (e.g., low labour costs for research and labour-intensive activities), or they might already supply minor weapons systems (e.g., small arms).

New arms entrants encounter criticisms. For example, the South African government's support for its attack helicopter (the Denel Rooivalk) was criticized as a grossly expensive white elephant designed to meet a terrorist threat when those terrorists were preparing to become the new government in a peaceful revolution and when the funds could have been spent on houses, schools and hospitals. However, supporters of the helicopter project claimed that it gave South Africa an independent military capability and created a core of engineers that helped Denel to win aerostructures contracts and resulted in the emergence of other new firms (e.g., Aerosud and Paramount). Furthermore, it was claimed that no country had made the transition from a developing to a developed economy without a thriving aerospace and defence sector (Morrison 2016). These are all arguments that can be addressed and evaluated critically by economists. They raise questions about the objectives of government policy, about the choice of projects, about the alternative use value of resources, and about the evidence of some of the claims and counter-claims. This book deals with such issues.

Conclusion

Contrary to popular belief, much is known about arms producers, but there are still substantial unknowns. The identity of the world's major arms firms and industries is known, as are their geographical distribution and their range of arms products. But the unknowns include the lack of official government statistics on the size and location of their national arms industries and their supply chains. Further unknowns include the lack of data on arms industries and arms R & D spending in nations such as China, Russia, India, Pakistan, Iran, Israel and North Korea. For all nations, arms R & D data are broad figures that fail to distinguish between spending on research and expenditure on development (e.g., R & D spending on nuclear weapons and their means of delivery). There is also a dearth of data on employment in arms R & D spending. For example, how many scientists, technologists and engineers are employed in arms R & D in the world's major arms producing industries and what are the alternative uses for such skilled labour? In the next chapter, the economics of arms industries is explained and assessed.

Notes

1. In the preface to his book, Scherer declared his doubts about writing a book on the economics of the weapons acquisition process. He was troubled by the basic premise of the book, namely, that efficiency is a desirable objective in the conduct of advanced weapons development and production programmes (Scherer 1964).
2. This figure is based on median share of equipment spending for NATO nations in 2015, where arms shares varied between 2 per cent and 35 per cent for member states. Some nations publish their national defence budget accounts showing details of arms spending but not all nations provide such details: hence, the use of total military spending as a first approximation of national arms spending. Two major sources of published data on various aspects of arms spending are the SIPRI yearbook and the SIPRI database, which provide data on world military spending, arms production and arms exports and other useful information.

3

THE ECONOMICS

Introduction

This chapter explains the economics of arms industries and their distinguishing economic features. All industries have economic features and the question we address here is, what are the *distinctive* economic features of arms producers and industries? The chapter starts by defining arms markets, some of the key facts about such markets and their distinctive economic features. These include their dependence on government and their distinctive supply-side features.

Arms markets

Industries form the supply side of a market that includes buyers. The competitiveness of a market is determined by the numbers of buyers and sellers. Large numbers of buyers and sellers form a competitive market, and this market provides a benchmark for assessing all markets and their industries. The opposite extreme arises where there is a single buyer or a monopsony buyer and a single seller or monopoly supplier.

Some markets are competitive, with large numbers of private buyers and private sellers. Examples of private competitive markets include agriculture, construction, household services (e.g., plumbing, window cleaning), motor vehicle repair and maintenance and some financial services. Within military markets, defence departments buy products and services such as accommodation, furniture, computers, telephones, motor vehicles and transport services that are also bought by large numbers of private consumers. Typically, most markets are characterized by large numbers of relatively small buyers, so they are competitive on the buying side of the market. Examples include large numbers of buyers of motor cars, televisions, fridges, washing machines, computers and mobile phones.

Arms markets are different on the buying side. Governments are the major, or only, buyer of arms (they are a single buyer, or monopsony). Only governments buy major lethal equipment (combat aircraft, missiles, tanks, warships). Potential buyers include the national government and any foreign governments that receive arms exports. But some arms might only be bought by the national government, which then becomes a monopsony buyer (e.g., nuclear-powered submarines in France, the UK and the US). As a result, the buying side of arms markets forms one of their distinctive economic features (see Chapter 4).

The supply side of arms markets can also be different, departing from competition. In many markets, the supply side has shown a long-run trend towards a smaller number of larger firms, with barriers to new entry. The result is industries that are far from competitive, comprising a small number of large firms, known as an oligopoly, or two firms forming a duopoly or a single monopoly supplier. An example of oligopoly is the US combat aircraft market (Boeing, Lockheed Martin and Northrop Grumman); there are duopolies in various civil aircraft markets (Airbus and Boeing for large jet airliners; Bombardier and Embraer for regional jet airliners); and monopoly suppliers include those supplying nuclear-powered submarines in the French and UK defence markets (DCNS in France and BAE Systems in the UK). Firms are either privately owned enterprises or they are state owned. Typically, arms firms in Canada, Germany, Japan, the UK and the US are privately owned while those in France (e.g., Nexter, DCNS), Italy (e.g., Leonardo), Spain (e.g., Navantia) and India (e.g., Hindustan Aeronautics, Indian Ordnance Factories) are state owned or partly state owned.

The extent of competition between suppliers will depend on the definition of the market: that is, whether it is defined as a national, regional or world market. Most European states have national monopoly suppliers for combat aircraft (e.g., Dassault Rafale in France, Saab Gripen in Sweden, Eurofighter Typhoon in Europe), but this market is competitive at the world level where there are substantial numbers of firms supplying combat aircraft (e.g., China, Russia, the US). Similarly, European states have national monopolies in main battle tanks, missiles, large military aircraft, warships and submarines but duopolies and oligopolies at the world level. Airbus is a European national monopoly for large military aircraft but a duopoly (with Boeing) in the world market for such aircraft. Within European states, warship building is represented by national monopolies that become oligopolies at the single European market level and competitive supply at the world level (e.g., Brazil, China, India, Russia, the US).

Rising costs

Arms are costly and, historically, unit costs have continued to rise. Norman Augustine famously claimed that when it comes to military aircraft, unit costs increase by a factor of four every ten years. Similar cost trends were identified for helicopters, commercial aircraft, ships and tanks, albeit with a lower rate of cost increase – a factor of two every ten years – for ships and tanks. These rising unit costs led to the forecast that by the year 2054, the entire US defence budget would purchase just one aircraft, and that aircraft would have to be shared 50:50 between the Air Force and the Navy, except for leap years when it would be available to the Marine Corp for the extra day (Augustine 1987: 143). Other analysts have recognized such rising unit costs and forecast a future with a single-tank army, a single-ship navy and just the Starship Enterprise for the air force (Kirkpatrick & Pugh 1983).

Rising arms costs reflect a technical arms race in which rival nations aim to establish an advantage over each other. A nation undertakes improvements in the weapons systems for its armed forces whenever it knows or believes that its rival is making improvements. Two or more nations become involved in an arms race where, say, improved armoured fighting vehicles, combat aircraft, missile defence systems and warships entering service in one nation increases the threat to its rival, thereby stimulating the rival to respond by buying similar modern equipment. Economists describe such rivalry as a tournament good (cf. professional sports such as tennis, European football and horse racing), where a nation maintains its military superiority by buying arms that are at the forefront of what is technologically possible and superior to those of its potential rival. In this rivalry, rising unit costs reflect the technical change between successive generations of arms, leading to cost escalation.

Typically, in civilian markets, competition and technical progress result in better products at lower prices, such as cheaper and better cars, fridges, washing machines, cameras, computers, televisions and mobile phones. In such civilian markets, consumer demands are limited by personal income levels, and competition between suppliers determines technical progress and the extent to which the benefits of such progress are reflected in lower prices. But such downward price trends in civilian markets are not reflected in defence equipment markets. Instead, arms are subject to rising unit costs, which is one of the industry's distinctive features. The technical arms race or tournament for lethal equipment is one explanation of rising unit costs for arms. The typical consumer good provides satisfaction to the consumer from its overall performance regardless of its performance relative to other users, whereas arms only provide benefits to their users where they are superior to their rivals' equipment. This has implications for costs. For example, the next-generation combat aircraft is more effective than its predecessor and will have both higher development costs and higher unit production costs. Higher development costs reflect technical progress, and fewer new projects mean greater "jumps" in technology between projects. Also, higher unit production costs mean fewer aircraft purchased from a limited defence budget, reducing the scope for learning economies and further increasing unit production costs (see below and Kirkpatrick (1995)).

The historical trend of rising unit costs of arms reflects both demand- and supply-side factors. On the demand side, armed forces demand the latest arms with funds provided by taxpayers. The armed forces are not subject to the hard budget constraints of private consumers with limited personal incomes. Instead, they seek to obtain the largest possible budget for their military service, operating a form of "Buggins' turn", whereby arms spending is shared between each of the services. For example, this year, the navy receives funds for its aircraft carriers; next year, the air force will receive funds for its latest combat aircraft; and then in the year after the army will receive funds for its latest tanks. The Buggins' turn principle resembles collusive behaviour in a cartel, with the major parties sharing the defence budget on an agreed basis rather than competing for the limited arms budget. As a result, each armed force accepts that with rising unit costs, its limited budget will be reflected in the purchase of smaller quantities of equipment. For example, the USAF originally planned to purchase 750 units of its F-22 combat aircraft but the final acquisition was for 187 operational aircraft. Silver bullet solutions are costly and have to be traded off against larger numbers of cheaper but inferior substitutes (e.g., small numbers of F-22 aircraft versus larger numbers of F-16 aircraft, reflecting a quality versus quantity choice).

The supply side of arms markets also leads to rising unit costs. Arms producers usually operate in non-competitive markets where supply is provided by a few firms (an oligopoly) or by one firm in the form of a monopoly. Such industrial structures lead to non-price competition, which is reflected in advertising, lobbying, product differentiation and technical progress with a general absence of price competition. Both arms producers and the armed forces have incentives to advocate "unrealistic costings" for new arms projects: underestimated costs and overestimated benefits means project approval by governments (Gray 2009).

Rising unit costs have attracted various policy solutions. Examples include increased exports to reduce unit costs, improvements in manufacturing technology and organization, reforms in government procurement and international collaboration. While such policies offer useful cost savings, they cannot offset the rising unit costs of arms: all nations' armed forces will have to recognize the continued historical trend of rising unit costs leading to smaller armed forces. The result of this is that economics becomes a determinant and a driver of disarmament.

Defining costs

Arms involve various cost categories over their life cycle, comprising acquisition, operations and support, and disposal costs. The resulting total forms the life cycle cost for a weapons system, where acquisition might account for almost 30 per cent of the total and operations and support might account for some 70 per cent (Navarro-Galera *et al.* 2011). For example, a new combat aircraft with acquisition costs of £20 billion will have life cycle costs of some £67 billion (including acquisition costs). Acquisition is further broken down into R & D and production costs. R & D involves feasibility studies, project definition and development (design, build, test and evaluation). Production involves investment in facilities and tooling, manufacture and acceptance tests. Operations and support involves personnel, fuel, transport and storage, training, spares, continuing design and modifications. Disposal involves transport and storage, dismantling, destruction, disposal and possible sales receipts. A UK study found that there is no unique life cycle cost associated with a specific item of defence equipment: instead, there is a range of life cycle costs dependent on the level in the defence equipment hierarchy at which costs are assessed (Kirkpatrick 2000: 364).

Disposal costs

Arms disposal is not always simple and costless. It varies from the simple and cheap to the complex and costly, with nuclear weapons disposal being at the latter end of the scale (e.g., clean-up and storage costs). Disposal arises where arms become "life-expired" due to obsolescence, rising maintenance costs, changes in operational requirements or the requirements of international arms control agreements. Disposal can be planned or unplanned and unexpected, where new technology makes some weapons systems and forces obsolescent or where a weapons system encounters unforeseen problems. For example, the UK's Valiant bombers were retired early (in 1965) due to unexpected wing fatigue and corrosion problems that would have required an expensive rebuilding programme. Some arms and other non-lethal defence equipment that become surplus to requirements might be sold to other national governments, while non-lethal equipment might be sold to private buyers (e.g., vehicles, military transport aircraft). Such sales provide revenue for the national government making the sale. Alternatively, some surplus equipment might be retained to provide a reserve in emergencies or to provide spares, but retention requires storage and involves costs of storage and making the site secure. Alternatively, surplus equipment might be sold for scrap.

Arms control agreements also involve the premature destruction of arms. Examples of such international agreements include the Treaty on the Non-Proliferation of Nuclear Weapons (1968), the Comprehensive Nuclear Test Ban Treaty (1996), the Intermediate Range Nuclear Forces (INF) Treaty (1987) and various bilateral agreements between the US and the former USSR to reduce their nuclear weapons stocks. The INF Treaty between the

US and the USSR eliminated all nuclear and ground-launched ballistic and cruise missiles with ranges of 500–5,500 km.

The destruction of weapons can be costly, especially when it comes to WMDs and nuclear weapons and forces. For example, the US has destroyed most of its chemical weapons at an estimated cost of $28 billion and, since 1992, it has spent a further $13 billion assisting former Soviet states to destroy their biological, chemical and nuclear weapons. Estimates suggest that it costs $3 billion for every 1,000 tonnes of chemical weapons destroyed (e.g., via incineration methods). Further costs arise for the inspection and verification of international arms control agreements. Such costs have to be compared with the costs of war.

Decommissioning and disposing of nuclear weapons and nuclear forces is extremely complex and costly. There are problems related to the safe disposal and storage of nuclear waste, and there are associated clean-up costs to make sites environmentally safe. The disposal task involves nuclear weapons, nuclear-powered delivery systems (e.g., submarines, surface warships), nuclear weapons storage facilities, and nuclear research and production plants. In some cases, apparently simple solutions have been adopted, such as the disposal at sea of nuclear-powered submarines (with environmental costs through contamination and pollution of sites). Examples include Russian submarine disposal in the Kara Sea (north of Siberia), the Kola Peninsula and storage at Vladivostok. The UK stores its decommissioned nuclear-powered submarines in Devonport and Rosyth, with storage of waste at Capenhurst, Cheshire. Data on costs are limited. For example, the cost of inactivating and scrapping a nuclear-powered submarine is estimated to be some $39 million (1995 prices (Kopte 1997)). For the UK, estimates of the costs for the environmental restoration of the military component of the Sellafield nuclear plant and site are estimated at some £35 billion (2016 prices (NDA 2016)).

What are the facts on costs?

Historical trends in unit costs can be used as a starting point in providing cost estimates for new projects. Evidence shows rising unit acquisition costs of defence systems for successive generations of equipment. The evidence also shows large, as well as rising, unit costs: modern arms are costly and their costs are rising. Table 3.1 shows examples of unit costs for UK fighter and bomber aircraft over the period 1940–2016. There is a clear trend of rising unit costs in real terms, with fighter aircraft unit costs rising by a factor of 178 since 1940! The introduction of jet-powered aircraft with the Meteor and Canberra led to higher absolute costs as well as further cost increases.

Table 3.1   Unit costs for UK military aircraft, 1940–2016.

Fighter aircraft	Unit costs (constant 2016 prices: £000s)	Bomber aircraft	Unit cost (constant 2016 prices: £000s)
Hurricane	186	Wellington	620
Spitfire	203	Lancaster	661
Meteor	490	Mosquito	328
Vampire	214	Canberra	1,535
Hunter	1,273	Vulcan	9,008
Lightning	4,198	Victor	5,709
Typhoon	33,051	Tornado	11,958

Notes. (i) Unit costs are for *airframe* unit production costs only, excluding costs of other components such as engines, undercarriage, radio, avionics, guns and missiles. (ii) Unit prices for Hurricane, Spitfire and Wellington based on contracts awarded in 1939/40, Lancaster and Mosquito contracts are for 1943, Meteor and Vampire contracts are for 1946, Canberra for 1951, Vulcan contract for 1954, Hunter and Victor contracts for 1955, Lightning contract for 1959, Tornado contract for 1979, and Typhoon contract for 2003. Constant prices based on UK Retail Prices Index. Source: DSTL (2010).

These levels of costs and their increases are not confined to military aircraft: they affect all types of air, land and sea equipment. Table 3.2 shows some examples. Not all arms are expensive: some are relatively cheap. A modern rifle, for example, has a unit production cost of £1,850, but older versions are available at £600 each; a modern machine gun has a unit cost of £4,300; and a grenade launcher has a unit cost of £1,230 (at 2016 prices). At the other extreme of the cost range is the planned new US B-21 Raider bomber, which is estimated to cost $23.5 billion to develop, with unit production costs of $564 million and a planned purchase of 100 units (Drew 2016). The examples in Table 3.2 show the cost levels of modern arms, ranging from

£5 million per unit for a tank to almost £7 billion for one aircraft carrier; and their costs continue to increase at a typical rate of 4 per cent per year (varying between 1 per cent and 10 per cent per year).

Table 3.2   Unit costs of all types of arms.

Type of equipment	Unit costs (constant 2016 prices: £ million)	Annual rate of increase (%)
Aircraft carrier	6,800	4
Air defence vessel	787	2
Anti-submarine warfare vessel	320	4
Nuclear-powered submarine (attack)	1,600	1
Diesel-powered submarine	370	3
Main battle tanks	5	6
Infantry fighting vehicle	5	4
Multiple rocket launcher	6	5
Combat aircraft	86	6
Bomber aircraft	370	10
Advanced jet trainer	21	4
Strategic transport/tanker aircraft	246	4
Electronic platform aircraft	443	2
Attack helicopter	30	5
Anti-submarine helicopter	25	6
Cargo/utility helicopter	20	4
Cruise missile	6	8
Ballistic missile	10	5
Reconnaissance UAV	6	6

Notes. (i) All costs are unit production costs except for naval vessels, which are unit acquisition costs, including development costs. Costs based on Pugh (2007) updated to 2016 prices using the UK GDP deflator. (ii) Figures are approximations and are rounded. For example, aircraft carriers range from large carriers to small carriers, where a small carrier might cost some £1.4 billion. Costs are based on worldwide examples of equipment but with a bias towards US and European designs. Some of the cost increase data – for aircraft carriers, anti-submarine vessels, combat aircraft and tanks – is based on Davies *et al* (2011).

Sources: Pugh (2007) and Davies *et al*. (2011).

Modern weapons systems involve both development and production costs. Most of the unit cost data in Table 3.2 refer to *unit production costs*. Development costs are a fixed cost, incurred whether one or more units are produced. Typically, for each class of defence equipment, development costs vary in proportion to unit production cost. Some examples are shown in Table 3.3. For example, the total development costs for a combat aircraft with a unit production cost of £100 million are some £10 billion. Total acquisition cost can be estimated using the following formula (Pugh 2007):

$$TAC = (R + Q) \times (upc)$$

where TAC is the total acquisition cost, comprising both development and total production cost, R is the ratio of development cost to unit production cost, Q is total quantity produced, and upc is the unit production cost. The same combat aircraft example with an output of 200 units would result in total acquisition costs of some £30 billion (cf. Typhoon). As a result, including development costs further increases the total acquisition cost of arms, making them even costlier. Other components of life cycle costs raise the cost magnitudes even further. For example, if acquisition costs are some 30 per cent of life cycle costs, then total life cycle costs for a purchase of 200 combat aircraft with a unit production cost of £100 million might be some £100 billion (over, say, a 50-year life cycle from project start to disposal).

Table 3.3 Relationship between development and production costs.

Class of equipment	Ratio of development to unit production cost (R)
Area-defence surface-to-air missiles	500
Armoured fighting vehicles	250
Artillery	150
Combat aircraft	100
Helicopters	120
Large fixed-wing aircraft	40

Note. Ratios shown are for completely new designs; variants of an existing type will involve lower ratios. Values are approximations.
Source: Pugh (2007).

Arms industries as decreasing-cost industries

Having emphasized the rising unit costs of arms, it seems contradictory to suggest arms industries are decreasing-cost industries. These two positions are reconciled by distinguishing costs *within* one type of equipment and costs trends *between* different generations of equipment. Decreasing unit costs refer to the impact on unit costs of a larger output of a *given type of equipment* (e.g., aircraft, tanks or warships; an example would be a larger output of Typhoon aircraft). In contrast, rising unit costs refer to cost trends between *different generations of equipment* or intergenerational equipment cost escalation (e.g., unit costs of a Spitfire compared with a Typhoon; or of a US Sabre jet compared with the F-35).

Decreasing unit costs are a further distinctive economic feature of arms industries. Decreasing unit costs result in falling unit costs as the scale of output increases, reflecting large fixed development costs together with economies of scale and learning economies. The decreasing unit costs found here differ from industries that are constant-cost industries, where unit costs do not fall with greater scale. There are also increasing-cost industries where above some relatively small scale, unit costs start to rise, reflecting dis-economies of scale (e.g., due to management problems as firms become larger).

Economies of scale determine industry structure, with decreasing unit costs leading to a smaller number of larger firms and oligopoly, duopoly or monopoly suppliers. Learning economies are another additional source of decreasing unit costs and are especially characteristic of the aerospace industry. Learning economies lead to falling unit costs as *cumulative* output increases. Take the example of an 80 per cent labour learning curve for aircraft. In this example, the first aircraft might require 1,000 man hours to complete; doubling output to two units means that the second aircraft requires 800 man hours to complete; a further doubling of output to four aircraft means that the fourth unit requires 640 man hours (80 per cent of the second unit); a further doubling to eight aircraft means that the eighth aircraft requires 512 man hours (80 per cent of the fourth). This example gives an 80 per cent labour learning curve showing that each doubling in cumulative output leads to a reduction in man hours of 20 per cent. Learning economies reflect greater experience and knowledge gained from repetition with greater output, and such economies are a major feature of aerospace industries. For example, greater output of UK jet fighter and bomber aircraft over the period 1945–60 resulted in reductions in unit costs ranging from 8 per cent to almost 80 per cent (Hartley 2014: 52). Learning economies have also been estimated for other arms industries such as warship building, where unit costs fell by some 10 per cent between the start of production and the production of the UK's 14th Type 23 frigate (Davies *et al.* 2011: 19).[1] While learning remains important, there have been some significant changes in manufacturing techniques, including the use of more capital-intensive production methods, resulting in fewer opportunities for labour learning (Hartley 2014).

Scale and learning economies lead to decreasing unit costs in production. In addition, large fixed development costs for many high-technology weapons are a further source of declining unit costs. These fixed development costs have to be shared across total output, meaning that unit total costs decline as output increases.

Various proposals have been made to allow aerospace firms to achieve greater output and lower unit costs from scale and learning economies as well as spreading fixed development costs over larger outputs. Proposals have included greater exports, international collaboration and joint arms programmes, where two or more services within a nation participate in the joint development and production of, say, a single aircraft or helicopter. The US F-35 Lightning II aircraft is a good example of a joint US programme. It is being bought by the US Air Force (1,763 units), the Navy (260 units) and the Marine Corps (420 units), giving a total planned US procurement of 2,443 units, which considerably exceeds the output for each service. Decreasing unit costs and the evidence on cost–quantity relationships has also encouraged firms to merge, thereby creating larger firms. Examples include Airbus, Boeing, BAE Systems and Lockheed Martin, where mergers have reduced the number of firms in an industry, with adverse effects on competition as oligopoly and monopoly have replaced competition (see Chapter 5).

The large firms are prime contractors that have extensive and complex supply chains providing parts, components and materials. Typically, firms in the supply chain are smaller, and operate in more competitive markets. However, price pressure and risk shifting from prime contractors to suppliers has led to some restructuring of supply chains. Examples include General

Electric's (US, aero-engines) acquisition of Smiths Aerospace (UK), Avio Aero (Italy) and Walter Aircraft Engines (Czech Republic). GKN Aerospace (UK) acquired Volvo Aero in 2012 and Fokker Technologies in 2015. The result is larger firms and less competition in supply chains.

Arms and strategic trade policy

Strategic industries have two interpretations, namely, military and economic. Militarily strategic industries are those arms industries that are regarded as "essential, key, vital components" of a nation's defence industrial base. The terms "vital", "essential" and "key" are usually asserted but rarely defined. Militarily strategic industries can be defined as those that provide a nation with independence, security of supply and resupply in conflict, arms tailored to the requirements of the nation's armed forces, and non-dependence on foreign monopolies. Examples of militarily strategic industries include nuclear-submarine building in Britain, France and the US and the associated nuclear weapons industries (Hartley 2014).

Economically strategic industries are different. They are decreasing-cost, oligopoly and high-technology industries reflected in their being R & D-intensive, with technical spillovers to the rest of the economy. Also, these are industries that are dependent on government, where government can use its procurement policy to protect "national champions" and maximize national economic benefits and rents. Economically strategic behaviour arises from the interactions between oligopoly firms in the world market, between oligopolies and national governments, and between different national governments. Strategic trade policy focuses on trade policy under oligopoly, where trade policies can raise national welfare by shifting monopoly profits from foreign to domestic firms through the use of policies such as subsidies to exports and R & D as well as import tariffs. In civil markets a classic example of an economically strategic industry and a strategic trade policy is the competition between Airbus and Boeing in the world market for large civil jet airliners.

Some arms industries also display the features of an economically strategic industry. Examples include military aerospace industries, specialist naval shipbuilding (e.g., aircraft carriers, submarines, frigates) and specialist land equipment firms (e.g., main battle tanks, armoured fighting vehicles, battlefield communications systems). These are sectors dominated by a small number of large arms producers with new entry limited by the costs of entry. Examples include BAE Systems, Lockheed Martin, Northrop Grumman, Raytheon, Dassault and Leonardo (formerly Finmeccanica). Governments are central to understanding national arms industries and the international arms trade. They actively support their national champions in competing for major arms export contracts (e.g., by waiving R & D levies, by trade missions and ministerial visits, and by limiting new entry). While strategic trade policy appears attractive, it has its critics. Some trade policies might protect special interest groups of producers and workers rather than benefit consumers and raise national economic welfare. Nor is it a simple task for government to estimate the optimal degree of trade protection or to identify potentially successful industries (they might back losers rather than winners). Economically strategic industries provide further economic benefits through technology spillovers.

Technical progress and spillovers

Technical progress has been a dominant feature of arms industries, resulting in new inventions, innovation, new products, industrial change and the emergence of completely new arms industries. For example, military combat aircraft did not exist in 1900, but by 2016 arms producers had developed high-speed combat aircraft, UAVs, guided missiles, intercontinental ballistic rockets and space systems. Other new arms industries emerging since 1900 include aircraft carriers, submarines, tanks, nuclear weapons and defence electronics (e.g., radar, battlefield communications). Major arms companies in 2016 that did not exist in 1900 included Airbus, Boeing, BAE Systems, Lockheed Martin, Northrop Grumman and Raytheon. The small numbers of large firms that are typical of arms industries tend to compete not on price but instead through non-price competition, including technical progress, product differentiation, advertising and political lobbying. Such non-price competition is a feature of arms producers in national and world markets. Governments have been central to the creation and development of arms industries through their military demands and state funding of major arms projects for their armed forces (e.g., aircraft carriers, nuclear submarines, combat aircraft, tanks, space satellites).

Technical progress has been a feature of arms producers and has been reflected in various performance indicators: for example, the increased speeds of combat aircraft, the greater effectiveness of weapons (e.g., the accuracy of cruise missiles), an increased ability to detect underwater submarines, and improvements in battlefield communications (e.g., mobile phones compared with carrier pigeons!). The demands from armed forces for improved weapons have led to firms expanding their R & D departments, employing larger numbers of scientists and engineers, which raises the costs of entry into the industry. As a result, arms producers are often R & D-intensive firms with governments funding the R & D efforts that have become a major feature of their competitiveness: arms firms compete on the basis of the technical aspects of their products rather than on the basis of price. For example, in July 2014, the USAF held a competition between a Boeing–Lockheed Martin team and Northrop Grumman for a new long-range bomber. Following the competition, in October 2015, the development contract was awarded to Northrop Grumman for the B-21 Raider bomber at a price of $564 million per unit. While unit price was not irrelevant in the competition, history confirms that unit prices at the start of a new advanced-technology weapons project are mostly uncertain and will rise. Typically, development contracts for new weapons projects are no longer on a fixed-price basis since arms producers cannot guarantee that they will be able to deliver at such an initial price for a project subject to considerable technical uncertainty. However, in the competition for the B-21 bomber, Northrop Grumman was believed to have significantly under-bid its rivals and committed to a fixed-price contract for the first five production lots for a combined 21 aircraft (Drew 2016). In competitive bidding, a contractor has incentives to "buy-into" a programme by submitting a low bid to achieve the benefits of the learning curve with the possibility of being able to undercut even more with the benefit of the experience gained from learning.

Not only are arms producers associated with technical progress, but some of their technologies spill over and spin-off to the rest of the economy. Examples include radar, the jet engine, civil airliners, the Internet, Formula 1 racing cars, unmanned air vehicles, health care management and composite materials (e.g., applied to bicycles, fishing rods and tennis racquets). Such technology spin-offs often provide a justification for state support of arms industries (e.g., strategic trade policy). While military spin-offs appear to be attractive, they are not costless and they are not the prime objective of defence spending (which is about peace, protection and security). Spin-offs raise important issues about the ownership of intellectual property: who owns the property rights in valuable ideas? In principle, ideas that have been funded by government are owned by the state, which has property rights in the revenue resulting from the sale of any marketable ideas. However, spin-offs are often developed and applied by civil firms outside the arms industry and it might not be worthwhile (because it would be too costly) for government to pursue their ownership rights into the rest of the economy (especially where civil firms might have used private funds to develop the ideas into marketable products).

But technology is changing and this is affecting the direction of spin-offs. Traditionally, spin-offs were from military to civil firms, but this direction is changing in two ways. First, there are greater spin-offs from civil to arms firms (e.g., IT, mobile phones). Second, there are major changes leading to a separation between military and civil technologies. For example, in aero-engines, each new development in jet engines was historically applied to civil aviation; but this traditional relationship is beginning to diverge. Future military needs are for new engine technology that can provide power and thermal capacity to service a new emerging class of laser weapons without sacrificing acceleration and sustained supersonic speed. In contrast, future civil aircraft require engine manufacturers to invest in fuel-saving technologies that have no immediate military application (*Flight* 2016).

Conclusion

Arms industries have some distinctive economic features. These include governments being the major or only buyers, an industry structure of monopoly or oligopoly, being decreasing-cost industries, being strategic industries, and having costs and barriers to new entry. Arms industries are also distinctive for their technical progress and associated technical spin-offs and spillovers. Next, the importance of government to arms industries is assessed.

Notes

1. Learning curves are represented by the formula: $y = aX^{-b}$, where y denotes direct labour hours per unit produced, X denotes cumulative output of a given type of aircraft, a denotes direct labour hours for the first unit, and b denotes the slope of the learning curve, usually defined in relation to a doubling of cumulative output. Cumulative output is total output produced (say, 1,000 aircraft over 10 years), whereas scale economies refer to annual output.

4

THE IMPORTANCE OF GOVERNMENT

Introduction: is the government to blame?

In addressing controversial problems, society and the media often seek to blame some individual, group or organization. For controversies associated with arms producers, governments are an obvious target for criticism. In response to the question of whose fault it is, the reply is often that the government is to blame! This chapter explores the role of government in arms industries. It assesses the importance of government and the validity of claims that "it is all the government's fault".

The role of government

Governments are central to understanding the arms market and arms industries. Their importance arises from their buying power, with government as either a monopsony or major buyer of arms, particularly of lethal equipment (including the supply of parts and components for such equipment). Examples include aircraft carriers, warships, nuclear-powered submarines, combat aircraft, missiles, tanks, armoured fighting vehicles and artillery, where national governments are often the only buyers of such equipment. As a single buyer, they are monopsony buyers. Exceptions arise where arms are exported, so there are also foreign buyers but the national government remains a major buyer of the equipment. In such cases the national government is not only a major buyer: it is also the original buyer that initiated and funded the project.

Governments can use their buying power to determine the size, structure, conduct, performance and ownership of both arms producers and arms industries. Buying power takes the form of arms contracts. National governments awarding arms contracts to their domestic arms producers and industries can determine the *size* of the arms industry: more contracts mean a larger domestic industry. For example, arms industries expand during wars and conflicts such as the First and Second World Wars, the Cold War, and the Korean, Vietnam, Afghanistan and Iraq conflicts.

Government can also use its buying power to determine the *structure* of its national arms industry through affecting the size of firms as well as the conditions of entry and exit from the industry. For example, major contract awards might be conditional on arms producers merging to create larger firms. An example occurred over the period 1958–60 when the UK government used its powers over contracts to restructure the UK aircraft industry, reducing the number of aircraft and engine firms to five major groups. Similarly, in late 1993, the US Department of Defense (DoD) informed its defence contractors that budget cuts required a major restructuring of the industry (at a dinner known as the Last Supper), leading to a wave of mergers, acquisitions and sales of defence businesses. Famous names such as General Dynamics, Grumman, Martin Marietta, McDonnell Douglas, Hughes and Rockwell were acquired by larger defence-focused firms: namely, Boeing, Lockheed Martin, Northrop Grumman and Raytheon. However, by 1998/99, the DoD prevented further major mergers on competition grounds, notably between Lockheed Martin and Northrop Grumman and between Newport News Shipbuilding and Ingalls Shipbuilding.

Governments further affect industry structure by allowing foreign firms to bid for national arms contracts (i.e. determining new entry) or by preventing or promoting industry exit through bailing out, or not bailing out, failing firms. For example, following the crashes of the early de Havilland Comet jet airliners, the UK government assisted the company's survival by purchasing some Comets as military air transports for the air force. Similarly, major operational problems with the UK Swift fighter aircraft led to its cancellation, with the Supermarine company only surviving because of UK orders for a reconnaissance version. Later, in 1958–60 when the UK aircraft industry was restructured, "candidates for relegation" were identified: namely, Supermarine and Gloster Aircraft, both of which exited the industry. Handley

Page, which refused to join the two newly formed aircraft groups, received no government funding nor any further military orders and finally exited the industry in 1970. In 1971, Rolls-Royce encountered problems developing the RB211 engine, and the aero-engine company was nationalized by the UK government to form Rolls-Royce (1971) Limited. Similarly, in the US, during the Korean War, the Curtiss-Wright aircraft company nearly disappeared because of its uncooperative attitude, which antagonized its major US military customers: apparently, it frequently demanded larger government subsidies. Vought, Republic and Fairchild left the military aircraft business because they failed to meet the design expectations of the air force and navy (Sapolsky & Gholz 1999).[1]

Government buying power also determines the *conduct* of arms firms, where conduct is reflected in the form of competition for arms contracts. Competition might be on the basis of price only or it might take non-price forms, such as the technical performance of arms (e.g., speed, range, fire power and weapons load of combat aircraft and tanks). Some contracts might be awarded on a non-competitive basis to a preferred domestic supplier. The successful firm might then receive a cost-plus contract, where there are no efficiency incentives and which provides the financial framework for cost overruns and delays. Competition appears to be an attractive solution, but where domestic markets are dominated by monopoly, governments aiming to promote competition have to be willing to open their domestic markets to foreign firms and buy from abroad (see Chapter 7).

Government further uses its buying power to determine industry *performance*, reflected in prices, productivity, profitability and exports.[2] Prices, productivity and profitability can be determined by using competition for the award of contracts where competition between rivals determines firm performance. Where competition is not possible, prices, productivity and profitability have to be negotiated and agreed (e.g., on the basis of "fair and reasonable" prices and profits), with government having the ability to regulate prices and profits. Government also determines exports through its choice of equipment for its national armed forces (e.g., whether such equipment meets the demands of foreign buyers); it affects export prices by requiring or waiving a levy on its R & D costs; it can provide favourable financial assistance to the buying nation; and, ultimately, it can agree to or ban export sales (e.g., of specific arms and/or to specific countries).

Government buying power can also be used to change the *ownership* of arms producers. It can decide between state and private ownership, choosing whether to nationalize or privatize all or certain arms producers. State ownership or nationalization means that arms producers can be required to act in the national interest, they can pursue objectives other than maximum profits and their prices and profits will reflect "wider" interests rather than the "narrow" commercial interests of private shareholders. In contrast, private ownership means that arms producers are subject to profit incentives, competition from rival firms and the "policing" role of private capital markets (threat of losses and takeovers), all of which will promote efficient outcomes. In the 1980s, the UK government privatized its arms industry, shifting from state-owned firms to privately owned ones. Privatizations included BAe (later BAE Systems), Rolls-Royce, the warship industry, the Royal Dockyards, the Royal Ordnance Factories and most of the Defence Evaluation and Research Agency (which later became QinetiQ).

In evaluating ownership issues, there is a tendency to compare models of perfect socialism with actual capitalism, or perfect capitalism with actual socialism, when the reality requires a comparison of two imperfect models of firm behaviour. For example, actual state-owned arms firms might pursue their own objectives, such as maximizing the number of high-technology arms development projects or maximizing employment or maintaining loss-making plants in high-unemployment areas. A regime of soft budget constraints will not be conducive to efficiency. Similarly, actual privately owned arms firms might seek to avoid competition and achieve monopoly power; they might pursue objectives other than maximum profits, such as a "quiet life" or maximizing managerial perks; and private capital markets might be imperfect, failing to fulfil their policing role so that outcomes might not be economically efficient. Private arms firms also depart from the perfect-capitalism model in that for major projects, they are dependent on government for financing. Why can arms projects not be privately funded?

Can the private sector fund arms projects?

It is often claimed that arms projects can and should be funded by the private sector, either from the internal funds of firms or through the capital market. Certainly, the private sector funds major high-technology, risky and long-term civil development projects, including the exploration of oil and gas fields (e.g., the UK in the North Sea), new pharmaceutical products, new models of motor cars, new types of computers, mobile phones and space satellites (for television and communications). Such projects are funded from a firm's own internal funds, or from external sources of funds either in the form of the capital market or from funds provided by other firms in the supply chain. Some arms projects are funded by the private sector, such as military outsourcing activities (e.g., training, support, facilities, air tanker operations, space communications). But for major arms projects, which are high technology, costly and require long development periods, government usually provides the necessary funding. Examples include aircraft carriers, warships, nuclear-powered submarines, combat aircraft, specialist military airlifters and special mission aircraft, missiles, tanks, armoured fighting vehicles and military space systems. Why are privately owned arms firms unwilling to fund such projects?

Arms projects in the form of lethal equipment can only be sold legally to government, which is the only buyer for the equipment. Effectively, government is the market and, in democracies, governments can change at an election and a new government might cancel major arms projects. Furthermore, many of the technologies, physical capital facilities and labour skills required to develop and produce the arms have no alternative uses (they are highly specific to arms industries). For example, government is the only buyer of nuclear-powered submarines, and the resources required to develop and produce such submarines have limited alternative uses (e.g., skilled labour might be used in the civil nuclear power industry). As a result, private firms will be unwilling to bear all the risks and costs of undertaking a major arms project. They will be concerned that they might never recover their costly and specific investments in the human and physical resources needed to develop and produce high-technology and costly arms projects (known as the "hold-up problem"). In these circumstances, government will be required to bear the costs and risks of funding arms projects.

The market for civilian high-technology projects is different. Private firms and capital markets are willing to fund such projects (e.g., exploration of oil and gas fields) because they are supplied to a genuine market comprising large numbers of private consumers, with market prices for products (unlike the single buyer in arms markets). Firms will have reasonable expectations (but not certainty) that the future market will be profitable. Private sector projects will not be so large as to risk the future survival of the firm, and the technology and resources required will have alternative uses and will not be specific to a single government buyer. Private arms firms can also "protect" themselves from some of the risks of the arms market by diversifying into other markets, such as other arms markets, civil markets and export markets.

Government, technical progress and spin-offs

The government's role as a major or only buyer also allows it to influence technical progress in arms industries. The government buys arms on behalf of its armed forces, who specify their requirements in relation to potential future threats usually reflected in the need for better air, land and sea equipment. For example, the speed of fighter aircraft increased from 65 miles per hour in 1914, to 355 miles per hour (Spitfire) in 1938, to 452 miles per hour in 1945 (Meteor jet), to 2,200 miles per hour in 1966 (US Lockheed SR-71). But technical progress is costly, leading to rising unit costs of arms between successive generations of equipment (the Augustine effect: see Chapter 3). Historically, in the 1930s, aircraft firms relied on prominent individual designers (e.g., R. J. Mitchell for the Spitfire, Willy Messerschmitt in Germany). Technical progress required firms to employ more scientists and technologists, creating larger design and development teams capable of solving the advanced technology demands of the government's armed forces. Governments provide the funds for such technical advances (Hartley 2014).

Arms technology demanded by a government's armed forces has a further dimension in the form of spin-offs. Technology spin-offs have been known by various names, including spillovers, externalities, diffusion and technology transfer. They involve the commercial application of arms technology to some other application either within the same firm or the same industry or within a civil firm in a different industry.

There are many examples of arms technologies spinning-off to other industries. Technical advances in military aircraft have been applied to civil aircraft. Examples include the jet engine, radar, flight control systems and new materials, which have been applied to Airbus, Boeing, Bombardier and

Embraer civil jet airliners. Some aerospace technologies have been applied in other industries such as Formula 1 racing cars and improved brakes for motor cars, and helicopter blade technology has been applied to the turbine blades used for wind farms. Jet engines have been used for marine propulsion. Other examples include the use of materials in fibre jackets for mountaineering, the use of glues in dentistry and injury treatments, and the development of new materials for bicycles, fishing rods and other sports equipment. There have been pioneering developments in surgery and the treatment of serious injuries, and the emergence of drones able to deliver books to people's homes. Defence uses opened up the space market through launchers and satellites, with satellites leading to developments in communications, television, mobile phones, navigation and weather forecasting. Equally impressive developments involved the Internet. The early development of the Internet was funded by the US Department of Defense, leading to major advances in computing and electronics and ultimately to worldwide economic benefits (e.g., time savings from improved communications, video-conferencing and access to knowledge). Israel provides a further example of spin-offs. Some staff from its Unit 8200 (a military intelligence unit) have left the unit and founded Israeli IT and other high-technology companies (e.g., Check Point, Indeni, Leadspace).

The examples of spin-offs from arms producers are impressive and have often been presented as a major argument for military spending. Such arguments need to be assessed critically. Interest groups favouring military spending have incentives to exaggerate claims about spin-offs. They will assert that the economic benefits of spin-offs are difficult to measure, but it might be that the difficulties of measurement arise because there is nothing to be measured! It also has to be recognized that spin-offs are an extra bonus of defence spending and not its main objective, which remains peace, protection and security for a society. Nor can it be assumed that arms producers are the only source of spin-offs: other industries might also generate spin-offs, some of which might be used by arms producers (i.e. spin-ins). Indeed, there are future possibilities of spin-ins from civil firms crowding out traditional arms producers. As a result, broadly commercial firms with a sideline in defence production might hold governments "hostage" if the price is not acceptable and the market is too small for a firm that is primarily a civilian producer. But similar hostage problems, acceptable prices and small defence markets arise with traditional arms producers too. Government has the option of responding to the "hostage" problem by threatening to import arms from foreign suppliers.

Spin-offs raise at least three problems for economists. First, a central issue concerns the market value of arms spin-offs. Major estimation problems arise because considerable lags can arise between the original development of an idea and its eventual application to the civilian economy. There is the associated task of identifying genuine causal relationships between the original technology and its applications, which have to be distinguished from the exaggerated claims of interest groups. Major challenges arise in placing a money value on spin-offs that are non-market outcomes, lacking market prices. Furthermore, there is the counterfactual issue of whether similar or better-technology spin-offs might be developed by other industries and, if so, at what cost (e.g., pharmaceutical and automotive industries).

Second, state intervention in private markets is often justified in terms of market failure. Applied to spin-offs, the key question is whether there are failures in arms R & D markets. One possibility is that R & D is risky and uncertain, requiring long time periods for development and involving possible spin-offs, making it costly to establish complete property rights in ideas: hence, the possibility that competitive markets will underinvest in research (development differs in that property rights are more easily and cheaply established). Even where failure in R & D markets is established, it does not follow that arms projects are the only and least-cost solution: other policies include changes to patent laws that establish property rights in valuable ideas and the correction of failures in private capital markets.

Third, questions arise about the transmission mechanism whereby arms technology spin-offs are transferred to other sectors of the economy. Spin-offs suggest that the technology is transferable with alternative uses. In contrast, some arms technology might be non-transferable: for example, stealth technology and some of the technologies required for nuclear-powered submarines (i.e. defence-specific technologies where there are no other users). Technologies are embodied in human and physical capital: namely, people and their skills and capital assets such as computers and machinery. On this basis, transmission mechanisms include labour turnover, where skills are transferred to other firms (e.g., arms workers moving to the car industry) or through science and engineering labour acting as consultants to other industries (e.g., Formula 1 racing cars); through the supply chain, with advanced technology from prime contractors flowing to small–medium-sized firms in the supply chain; and through links with universities (e.g., university science parks (see Hartley 2014)). However, arms spin-offs might be restricted by military secrecy, which can prevent transfers.

Can arms producers reduce their dependence on government?

Arms producers can reduce their dependence on *national* governments in a variety of ways. They might export arms to *foreign* governments, they can move from being a single arms producer to a multi-product arms producer, or they can diversify into civil markets. History provides many examples of arms producers adjusting to change following major wars, disarmament and technical change. Wars result in an increased demand for arms, requiring an expansion of arms industries and leading to new entrants and increased capacity for existing producers. In contrast, the end of conflict leads to disarmament, which is associated with exits from the industry and industrial rationalization and consolidation through mergers and acquisition (see Chapter 9). Technical progress also affects the size and structure of arms industries, leading to new entry, diversification for existing producers and, in some cases, the creation of completely new industries (e.g., aerospace, electronics (Hartley 2011a, 2014)).

All firms have to choose a market. Private-enterprise firms will select the most profitable markets, with shareholders determining the success of their choices: shareholders will invest in a firm so long as it offers profits at least equal to the returns in the next-best alternative use, adjusted for risk. Privately owned arms firms are no different from other firms: they have to select a "core" business that is potentially profitable. State-owned enterprises are not subject to profit-maximizing objectives, although they might be required to act commercially. Regardless of ownership, arms producers have to allocate their resources between arms and civilian markets. Some might prefer to become arms specialists with arms as their core business. Other firms might have different views about the profitability of various markets and their comparative advantages (i.e. their business strengths or what they are good at). Some state-owned firms might be limited by law to operating in specific arms markets and prevented from operating in other markets. The key aspect of privately owned firms is their responsibility for selecting the firm's best markets. Their entrepreneurs have the task of using their judgement to respond to uncertainty, where no one can predict the future accurately. If they guess correctly, they will make money and survive; if they make mistakes, they might have to exit the industry. But arms markets are different from civilian markets. They are dependent on government as a single or major buyer that specifies its requirements; compare this with civilian markets where there are large numbers of private buyers each with different and uncertain demands. The importance of government in arms markets means that producers have incentives to lobby for contracts, with their lobbying efforts focused on a single buyer. This dependence on a single buyer also provides incentives for arms producers to diversify their business to ensure that they are not completely dependent on a government buyer (see Chapter 8).

Arms producers can diversify their business in a variety of ways. They might choose to specialize in arms as a single-product or multi-product arms firm supplying a variety of national and international arms markets. Examples include MBDA, a European manufacturer of missiles; DCNS (France), a naval specialist supplying surface warships and submarines with further interests in energy (64% state owned); and Nexter (France), which specializes in land systems (state owned; it merged with Krauss-Maffei (Germany) in 2015). Examples of multi-product arms firms include BAE Systems (UK), which supplies air, land and sea systems (privately owned); Lockheed Martin (US), which is involved in aerospace, defence, security and advanced technologies (privately owned); and Northrop Grumman (also US), which specializes in aerospace, mission systems (including electronics) and technology services (privately owned). In some examples, the range of company divisions reflects the development of new businesses for traditional arms producers (e.g., security, cyber, mission systems and technology services).

Arms producers also reduce their dependence on governments by diversifying into civilian markets, where there are often large numbers of private buyers. Examples of firms less dependent on government include Airbus and Boeing, each as aerospace specialists with major military and civil markets, and also some of the major jet engine firms (e.g., Rolls-Royce (UK), Safran (France)). Arms producers also diversify by creating industrial conglomerates with a variety of unrelated activities. General Electric is a US multinational conglomerate with a military and civil aero-engine business and a variety of civil businesses that are often acquired by buying established firms (e.g., financial services, power generation, household appliances, medical imaging). Leonardo (formerly Finmeccanica) was a similar conglomerate with aerospace and defence activities together with a range of other civil businesses including rail, bus and energy companies. However, by 2016 these other companies were divested, allowing Leonardo to specialize in its core businesses of aircraft, helicopters, space, defence and security electronics.

Creating competition among buyers?

Arms markets are not like normal commercial markets where there are large numbers of buyers and sellers. Instead, arms markets have only one buyer, in the form of the national government. Even where the arms producer wishes to export its equipment to other governments, it will need government approval and often its assistance for marketing and supporting its export sales. A single buyer will dominate arms suppliers regardless of the number of suppliers. Every supplier has to respond to the demands of the monopsony buyer or exit the market. The single buyer will specify its technical requirements, it will determine the extent of competition in the market, and it will provide the funding for retaining excess capacity in the arms industry. Vote-sensitive politicians with arms plants in their constituencies will support the retention of excess capacity in arms industries.

Conventional economic analysis regards government monopsony in arms markets as a given, not to be questioned. In reality, competition can be introduced into the demand side of arms markets, creating buyer-side rivalry for the acquisition of arms (Sapolsky & Gholz 1999). Competition on the buying side of the market can be actual or simulated. Proposals for real rivalry between the armed forces is a novel initiative when all the pressures are for a shift away from inter-service rivalry.

Centralized procurement appears attractive since it removes so-called costly duplication and waste of resources. Under centralized procurement, each military service will avoid rivalry and support a "joint" arms programme (e.g., US F-35 aircraft supported by the US air force, navy and marines as well as by Britain). In contrast, the intention of real inter-service competition is to expose fundamental differences between the services about military priorities, combat doctrines and the relative effectiveness of different technology options and alternative weapons programmes. For example, the army and air force can express their views on the navy's plans for new aircraft carriers, while the army and navy can be equally critical of the air force plans for a new strategic bomber, and the navy and air force can be critical of the army's plans for a new state of the art tank. Such inter-service rivalry will identify costs and trade-offs to the defence secretary faced with choosing between these alternative weapons projects (or none!). Instead, the alternative of centralized procurement promotes collusive behaviour between each of the armed forces, with acceptance of the principle of Buggins' turn in arms procurement. Such collusion will fail to pursue dynamic organizational and technological competition aimed at providing optimal solutions to defence problems. But the dangers of small numbers of services with potential for collusion remains. The challenge facing any defence secretary or minister is to create an organizational structure that promotes real inter-service rivalry. This might be achieved by introducing hard budget constraints for each service, probably in the context of cuts in military budgets. The prospect of budget losses will provide a stimulus for each military service to present the minister with more accurate data on trade-offs.

Conclusion

This chapter has shown that governments are important to arms industries. Their buying power determines the size, structure, conduct and performance of the industry. Governments can also determine ownership by either privatizing or nationalizing the industry, either in part or totally. As a result, government has some responsibility for its arms producers, but such responsibility is subject to at least two major limitations.

First, in democracies, governments are elected and re-elected and their policies reflect the preferences of their electorates. Admittedly, there are limitations on the ability of different electoral systems to reflect the preferences of citizens (e.g., general elections versus referenda). Second, arms producers are not completely passive: they have some power in that they can influence the policies of governments through lobbying for contracts, subsidies, preferential purchasing and protection from foreign competition. The next chapter explains and evaluates the supply side of arms markets.

Notes

1. In the civil aircraft field, in 2016 the Canadian aerospace company Bombardier received provincial and federal state support in the form of repayable loans to continue development of its new jet airliner. In this form, state support for civil aircraft might enable arms producers to survive.
2. Civil aircraft provide an example of government support affecting industry performance. In September 2016 the WTO found that the EU had failed to eliminate subsidies (repayable launch investment) to Airbus that were previously found to have violated trade rules. It was estimated that total subsidies of almost $22 billion were paid to Airbus, resulting in lost US exports and lost US jobs (estimated lost sales of 375 Boeing aircraft (WTO 2016)).

5

ARMS INDUSTRIES: STRUCTURE AND CONDUCT

Introduction: overview

Arms industries form the supply-side of arms markets. Typically, the major arms producers are large firms forming national monopolies, duopolies or oligopolies. US arms firms dominate the world industry (see Chapter 2). Examples include Lockheed Martin, Northrop Grumman and Raytheon, and they often operate in *national* oligopoly industries. European rivals include Airbus, BAE Systems, Leonardo and Thales, with these companies usually being *national* monopolies. In terms of firm size, a distinction can be made between absolute and relative size. Absolute size deals with firm size measured by absolute sales and employment numbers, whereas relative size focuses on firm size relative to the market or industry. For example, a large number of absolutely large and similar-sized firms forms a competitive industry compared with one absolutely large single supplier forming a monopoly.

Ownership differs between nations. Privately owned arms producers are typical of the US, the UK, Germany and Sweden. State-owned arms producers are typical in Brazil, Italy, China, India, Israel, Russia and South Africa. France has a mixed ownership model with variations of private and state ownership (but traditionally, state ownership has dominated). Public ownership is also typical for procurement agencies providing research advice to national governments, but the UK is an exception in that most of its former government research agencies have been privatized: QinetiQ is privately owned but the Defence Science and Technology Laboratory (DSTL) remains state owned.

Industry structure facts

Arms industries are continuously changing in size, structure and the organization of firms. War and peace have resulted in larger and smaller arms industries, respectively. Mergers, acquisitions, new entry and exits have affected industry structure. Company names often change and firms frequently change how their businesses are organized.

An example was the 1993 restructuring and reorganization of the US defence industry, which was characterized by mergers, acquisitions and exits. New names such as Lockheed Martin and Northrop Grumman emerged, while other names remained unchanged even though there were major acquisitions. For example, Boeing acquired McDonnell Douglas and Rockwell but retained its Boeing name. Raytheon acquired Chrysler Defence Electronics, Hughes Aircraft and part of Texas Instruments. Since 1993 there have been further changes, such as the 2015 Lockheed Martin acquisition of Sikorsky Aircraft (helicopters), which retains its name and is part of Lockheed Martin's Mission Systems and Training business segment. Over time, arms producers also change the organization of their businesses. Raytheon, for example, is organized into five business divisions: Integrated Defence Systems; Intelligence, Information and Services; Missile Systems; Space and Airborne Systems; and Forcepoint (cyber security).

A further example of restructuring and name change involved the (state-owned) French group Nexter and the (privately owned) German firm Krauss-Maffei Wegman (KMW), which merged in 2015 to create a new group known as KNDS. This group represented consolidation in the European land systems industry.

Typically, arms industries are dominated by a declining number of larger firms forming national monopolies, duopolies and oligopolies. The world's five largest arms firms are shown in Table 5.1. US firms specializing in aerospace or in supplying a range of air, land and sea systems dominate the top five.

Table 5.1 World's top five arms producers, 2015.

Company	Specialism	Arms sales (US$m)
Lockheed Martin	Ac, H, El, Mi,Sp	36,440
Boeing	Ac, H, El, Mi, Sp	27,960
BAE Systems	A, Ac, El, MV, Mi, SA, Sh	25,510
Raytheon	El, Mi	21,780
Northrop Grumman	Ac, El, Mi, Ser, Sp	20,060

Notes. (i) Specialisms are for arms only. Civil sales are not shown. For example, Boeing has a major civil aircraft business, which would classify the firm as an aerospace specialist. (ii) A = artillery; Ac = aircraft; El = electronics; Mi = missiles; MV = military vehicles; SA = small arms and ammunition; Ser = services; Sh = ships; Sp = space. Source: SIPRI (2016a).

Monopoly and competition are determined by the number of firms in a market and by the definition of the market. National monopolies become competitive firms in world markets. Monopolies are single or sole suppliers in the national market, but they might be one among a larger number of suppliers once the market is defined to embrace the world. Examples are shown in Table 5.2. Combat aircraft forms an oligopoly industry in the US but is competitive at the world level. In contrast, strategic bombers are a monopoly supplier in the US but form an oligopoly in the world market. In some markets the threat of entry controls monopoly power (i.e. reflected in contestable markets). Elsewhere, in markets for submarines and tanks, there are large numbers of suppliers at the world level.

For simplicity, competition is defined by the number of sellers, but this definition departs from the economist's model of competitive markets, which also focuses on entry conditions and assumes free entry. Governments determine entry to arms industries and markets through their buying power and the ability to award arms contracts. They determine whether national or foreign arms firms are allowed to bid for arms contracts. Ownership also matters in that government will be more willing to subject privately owned firms to competition, while they will be less willing to subject state-owned firms to national and foreign competition. Technical progress can also change entry conditions, with new technology allowing new firms to enter arms industries (e.g., UAVs led to new entrants).

The facts of the structure and conduct of arms industries will be analysed starting with the traditional approach. Arms industry performance is assessed in Chapter 6.

Table 5.2 Monopoly and competition in national and world markets.

	Number of major arms producers				
Arms market	*US*	*Europe*	*Russia*	*China*	*Rest of the world*
Combat aircraft	3	6	2	1	2
Strategic bombers	1	0	1	1	0
Attack helicopters	3	2	2	2	1
Large military transport aircraft	2	1	2	2	2
Submarines	2	7	1	1	2
Tanks	2	10	2	1	9

Notes. (i) Numbers of arms producers are illustrative rather than comprehensive. The table is based on the author's broad assessment of markets. (ii) For large military transport aircraft, Ukraine is included under Russia. (iii) Actual numbers of firms shown, excluding potential entrants. For example, strategic bombers shows one US firm but omits potential entrants in the form of Boeing and Lockheed Martin.

The traditional approach

Traditionally, industrial economists analysed industries using their structure–conduct–performance paradigm (SCP paradigm). In this model, industry structure determined performance, although allowances were made for "feedback", with performance determining structure. Structure is measured by the number and size of firms and by entry conditions. Conduct embraces various aspects of price and non-price competition used by firms (e.g., advertising, R & D, marketing and sales effort). Performance is measured in various ways, including prices, exports and profitability. However, economics applies a strict definition of performance in terms of gains and losses from policy changes. Using this approach, a desirable economic change occurs when at least one person is made better off and no one is made worse off, and the best or optimum position occurs where it is impossible to make one person better off without making someone else worse off (known as a Pareto optimum). These conditions for a desirable economic change are demanding, since most changes involve gainers and losers.

An alternative criterion compares gainers and losers with opportunities for compensation. The alternative compensation approach to identifying a desirable change requires that the potential gainers from a change should be able to overcompensate the potential losers. For example, if change leads to one individual being $1,000 better off and another person being $1 worse off, then the potential gainer from the change is able to compensate the loser and still be better off (i.e. overcompensation is possible). Whether actual compensation is paid will depend on society's views about the desirable distribution of income.

The economist's model of perfect competition achieves the best or optimum allocation of resources for an economy. This optimum leads to both *technical efficiency* and *economic efficiency*. Technical efficiency arises because competition between firms means that each firm has to adopt the most efficient and cost-minimizing production methods to survive and remain in business (also known as X-efficiency). Economic efficiency arises because firms will produce precisely what consumers require, expressed by their willingness to pay a price that reflects the extra costs of production. The result is economically efficient since any further change will only make someone better off at the expense of making someone else worse off. In other words, where the "correct" goods and services are being made in the "correct" quantities and are allocated to the people who value them most highly, there is no scope for any further efficiency gains. This model is used to assess actual economies and their performance in terms of major market failures and the extent of their departure from the "ideal" of perfect competition. Market failures identify where economic problems arise, their causes and how to improve the performance of the economy in question (Harford 2007: Chapters 3 and 4).

Markets fail where there are monopolies, externalities, information problems and public goods. Monopolies charge high prices that exceed their extra costs of production, they earn high profits and they prevent new entry. Externalities mean that prices do not reflect the costs and benefits for society, resulting in provision of "too much" undesirable activity (e.g., pollution, noise, traffic congestion) and "too little" socially desirable activity (e.g., flood control, R & D). Information failures arise where some decision-makers (namely, consumers, producers or governments) might lack sufficient information for beneficial trading and exchange. There might be rigged markets, where some traders have valuable "insider information". Examples include insider information on future share issues, or cartels affecting prices at auctions (e.g., antiques, houses), or the used car market, where sellers know more than buyers about the quality of their used cars, and badly treated cars are termed lemons (an adverse selection problem). Further information problems arise with insurance markets, where insurance cover might encourage reckless behaviour (moral hazard).

Public goods differ from private goods. Goods such as defence, peace, police, and street lighting are characterized by non-rivalry and non-exclusivity. These are goods where my consumption of the good is not at the expense of your consumption and I am unable to prevent you consuming the good. For example, my consumption of defence and peace is not at your expense, and once defence and peace are provided I cannot prevent you from benefiting from these goods. No mechanisms exist to allow consumers to express their willingness to pay for such public goods, and individuals have incentives to free ride on others' willingness to pay.[1] An example arises in NATO, where the US often complains that most European nations "free ride" on US defence spending.[2]

A further aspect of market failure associated with Keynesian economics can be mentioned. Keynes recognized that economies can settle at a position of underemployment or unemployment equilibrium. In such circumstances, state intervention is required to raise aggregate demand in the economy, leading to greater output and increased employment. Aggregate demand can be raised through higher government spending and lower taxation. For example, a government might increase its spending on public sector projects such as roads, bridges, tunnels, hospitals and schools, or it could increase spending on new arms and space projects.

Identifying market failure provides an understanding of the causes of economic problems and the possible policy solutions that are available to improve economic performance. Care is needed in identifying market failure: what appears to be a failure might reflect markets working correctly and efficiently in a world of scarcity. For example, buyers and sellers often find solutions to information problems through such devices as branding reputations by firms, guarantees against faulty products, and search processes by consumers and workers (e.g., websites and expert information provided by consumer groups). The fact that such activities involve costs does not represent market failure. Indeed, market operations are not costless and involve transaction costs: the costs involved in undertaking market transactions. For example, firms are viewed as institutions that economize on transaction costs, including the costs of handling information and agreeing contracts with suppliers and workers. Over time, firms change as new technologies and new opportunities emerge for reducing transaction costs. As a result, the arms firm of 2016 differs from that of 1945 and 1900. Nor does market failure necessarily imply that state intervention is beneficial: the costs of government intervention may be larger than the costs of market failure, particularly since government failure is not uncommon. Consider the application of market failure analysis to arms markets.

Failures in arms markets

Arms markets depart substantially from the economist's competitive model, with failures on both the demand and supply sides of the market. The demand side is dominated by a major or single buyer (the government) rather than a large number of competing private buyers. The government can use its buying power to determine the size, ownership, structure, entry and exit, conduct and performance of arms industries and markets. Governments also possess insider information about their demands for arms, leading to information asymmetries. They know what they wish to buy, when they want to buy it and in what quantities, and they know about their willingness to pay and the definition of the market (i.e. willingness to buy from abroad). The result is government as the source of failure on the demand side of the market.

Failures also exist on the supply side of arms markets. Arms industries are usually dominated by monopolies and oligopolies that are privately owned or state owned. Private monopolies and oligopolies might pursue objectives other than maximum profits (e.g., a quiet life, managerial perks), leading to X-inefficiency. There are likely to be barriers to new entry so that new firms will face obstacles to entry that restrict the opportunities for more resources to flow into potentially profitable arms markets. Costs are one major entry barrier, where high costs are required to compete with established firms. For example, entry barriers arise from the need to employ large numbers of costly scientists, technologists and engineers for the development of high-technology weapons and it is also necessary to invest in costly and highly specialized plant and equipment. Market imperfections mean that competition is likely to be based on non-price variables as well as prices, so departing from the price competition of the competitive model. Competition in arms markets will take the form of R & D, product differentiation, advertising and lobbying, with price adding a further element in the competitive process. Governments often regulate the behaviour of private arms firms through their selection of contracts for the procurement of arms, their willingness to buy from abroad, their assessment of a firm's cost levels and their limits on the profitability of arms contracts.

Governments determine entry and exit from arms industries. They can decide which arms firms will receive defence contracts and they can bail out firms that they wish to retain in the national arms industry. A government's willingness to buy from abroad also determines industry structure by allowing foreign firms to compete with national monopolies and oligopolies or by preventing them from doing so. Where national markets are protected from foreign competition, the result is a private or state monopoly or oligopoly confronting a single government buyer. The limiting case is where a single or monopsony buyer negotiates with a monopoly supplier (known as a bilateral monopoly), where the parties might act as adversaries or partners, with the buyer seeking the lowest possible price and the seller seeking the highest possible price (cf. wage negotiations between a single employer and a trade union). The result is a bargaining outcome that might be far removed from the competitive model.

State ownership of arms firms means that governments are directly involved on both the demand and supply sides of the market. They can determine the objectives of state-owned firms (e.g., imposing non-profit objectives), efficiency levels (e.g., employment targets), prices and profitability. Where there are "soft" rather than "hard" budget constraints, state-owned enterprises are likely to be X-inefficient, and entry barriers mean no threats from new entry. Furthermore, state-owned arms firms will be protected from competition by rivals and will not have to respond to the incentives of private capital markets (threats of takeover and bankruptcy). The result is a state-owned arms firm negotiating with itself as a buyer, which is unlikely to resemble the efficiency of a competitive model.

In addition to monopoly problems, failures in arms markets arise from externalities and information problems. Some of the weapons produced by arms firms generate negative externalities in the form of noise from military aircraft and firing ranges as well as pollution and other hazards from nuclear weapons sites (involving substantial clean-up costs). But, there are possible beneficial externalities from technical spin-offs from defence R & D as well as from the armed forces supplying skilled labour to the civilian economy. Arms markets are also subject to information failures, reflected in information asymmetries and moral hazard. Asymmetries arise where privately owned arms producers are experts on their production possibilities and on the amount of effort to be given to a contract. As buyers, governments also have insider information when negotiating with arms contractors. Moral hazard is present where arms firms might believe that they are too important to be allowed to fail. However, state ownership might change some of the information failures that arise under private ownership. In principle, state ownership changes the insider position for both buyer and seller: governments as buyers might be more willing to reveal their true requirements to a state-owned firm, and a state-owned seller might be more willing to reveal its knowledge of its production costs. Moral hazard could be more likely under state ownership, with public firms believing that they are guaranteed arms contracts in perpetuity.

If arms markets are likely to depart significantly from the competitive model, why focus on market failure? There are two answers. First, the economic problems of arms markets can be reduced by applying the principles of competitive markets – namely, greater competition, regulation of monopoly power, competitive auctions and the application of incentive schemes – to arms contracts. Public policy might aim to simulate competitive markets and their outcomes. Second, the alternative to markets is some form of government solution; but while private markets can fail, so too can governments. Effectively, arms markets are political markets dominated by government as a buyer, regulator or owner. But even political markets do not solve the problems of market failure: monopoly, externalities, information and public goods problems still have to be addressed (Laffont & Tirole 1993; see also Chapter 8).

An alternative approach: the role of business strategy and firm conduct

Economists' traditional SCP model has been modified to recognize the role of business strategy and its impact on industry structure. In this modified model, structure is determined by a firm's strategic decision-making, from which follow conduct and performance. With this approach, strategy determines structure: structure does not just exist, it comes into existence from a firm's strategic decision-making. Critics of the SCP paradigm claim that it places too much emphasis on industry structure while under-emphasizing the role of firm conduct, from which inferences can be made about market structure. Emphasis has shifted from structure towards conduct, reflected in strategic decision-making by individual firms, where interdependence affects their conduct and behaviour.

More generally, strategic behaviour by individuals, groups, firms and governments has involved the application of game theory, leading to "new" developments in various branches of economics, including the New Industrial Economics (Romp 1997; Lipczynski *et al* 2009). Game theory is based on mutual interdependence, where the actions and welfare of one player are determined by the actions of other players in the game. A player could be an individual, a firm, an employer, a trade union or a government, and two players are needed for the interdependence required to play a game. The notion of mutual interdependence means that players now have incentives to act strategically by considering the effects of their actions on others. Mutual interdependence departs from the traditional assumption of independent individuals whose actions have no effect on the behaviour of others. Interdependence changes this assumption by allowing a player's welfare to depend on the actions of others, which can lead to possible market failures and economic inefficiency. Examples include the prisoner's dilemma game, where self-interest leads to an economically inefficient outcome.[3] The prisoner's dilemma game has been used to explain a two-nation arms race. Faced with a choice between mutual arms limitation and mutual arms escalation, each nation escalates its military spending rather than selecting the economically efficient outcome: mutual arms limitation (Sandler & Hartley 1995: 75).

Game theory is also used to analyse the behaviour of firms in duopoly and oligopoly industries and the use of pricing, output and merger policies to deter new entry into monopoly markets. Such examples are applicable to arms industries and firm conduct in the form of pricing, advertising, product differentiation and R & D strategies. Arms firms with both military and civil markets might price discriminate between these markets: for example, higher prices might be charged for a military version of a civil transport aircraft. Conduct also involves acquisition strategies where a firm acquires its rivals (thereby affecting industry structure). A further example of game theory and its relevance to arms producers arises with strategic trade policy in oligopoly markets. In this example, through strategic trade policy a government might be able to improve the competitive position of domestic firms against foreign rivals, leading to rent-shifting from the foreign to the domestic economy. Strategic trade policy involves the government targeting export promotion by a specific industry, such as the arms industry, the computer or pharmaceutical industry, or the large jet airliner industry (e.g., Airbus and Boeing).

Game theory has major applications to arms industries. These are often duopoly or oligopoly industries, or where they are monopolies, there will be interaction between the monopoly supplier and the government monopsony buyer. In arms markets, bargaining between suppliers and government occurs over the award of contracts and the negotiation of prices and profits for such contracts. Contract bargaining provides opportunities for both buyer and seller to engage in various game strategies such as bluff, chicken and brinkmanship, where each party seeks to obtain the best deal. The government buyer will seek to minimize the price paid, while the arms supplier will seek the highest possible price and profits. Both parties have to decide whether to agree or disagree and either or both can refuse to accept a trade. The ultimate sanctions are for government to cancel a project and for private arms suppliers to withdraw from the market.[4]

Market failure in arms markets might require some form of state regulation to improve the operation of markets. Regulation can take the form of structural and/or conduct regulation. Structural regulation is based on industry structure and might involve the break-up of monopolies, the prevention of mergers that might create monopoly, and choosing whether to allow or prevent new entry from foreign arms firms. Regulation of firm conduct influences the behaviour of firms by controlling prices, advertising, marketing, R & D expenditures, political lobbying and profitability (e.g., through price cap and rate of return regulation).

Conduct

The conduct of arms firms is reflected in the form of competition used in national and world markets. Typically, both price and non-price competition is used when bidding for contracts. National governments have different arms requirements and varying regulatory rules, all of which affect the mix of price and non-price competition used by national arms producers. When bidding in foreign arms markets, there is more emphasis on price and on the industrial benefits of procurement. For example, arms exporters will offer attractive deals, with promises of technology transfer and work-share (offsets: see Chapter 6).

Examples of various aspects of firm conduct occurred with the award of two UK contracts to Boeing in July 2016. In the competition to provide a new Apache attack helicopter for the UK army, Boeing reportedly reduced the price of its helicopters in an effort to win the contract against its rival for the contract: namely, AgustaWestland, which has a plant in the UK (now Leonardo Helicopters). The UK purchase of Apache helicopters "off-the-shelf" from Boeing meant that it shared in the scale economies from a large US order. The contract award included initial support for maintenance of the new helicopter plus spare parts and training simulators for UK pilots. At the same time, the UK also awarded a contract to Boeing for the supply of nine Poseidon P-8 maritime patrol aircraft, with Boeing allocating work to the UK creating up to 2,000 new UK jobs (with a contract value of some £3 billion over ten years). UK work included the development of the P-8 air base at Lossiemouth in Scotland, with work also awarded to UK suppliers such as Marshall, Martin Baker and General Electric.

Another dimension of conduct: bribery and corruption

Some aspects of non-price competition, including bribery and corruption, are illegal. Bribery involves offering rewards, either in cash or in kind (e.g., free holidays, free motor cars), to gain an illicit trading advantage. Similarly, corruption is an abuse of a position of trust to gain an unfair trading advantage. Basically, bribery and corruption distort normal competitive processes, leading to a misallocation of resources for both buyers and sellers in market transactions. Some governments have anti-bribery and corruption legislation, involving fines and imprisonment (e.g., the 1999 OECD Anti-Bribery Convention).

Examples of bribery and corrupt practices have arisen in the arms industry (e.g., at BAE Systems, Boeing, Lockheed Martin and Leonardo, and in China's arms industry (Chase *et al* 2015)).[5] But the arms industry is not among the worst industries when it comes to bribery and corruption: the leading industries include construction, extraction, transport and IT/communications. Examples of firms prosecuted for bribery and corruption include Daimler (Germany) for using bribes to sell its vehicles to governments in China, Nigeria, North Korea and Vietnam; Lucent Technologies (US), which paid for Chinese officials to visit Las Vegas and elsewhere in a bid to win contracts; and Titan (US), which was prosecuted for bribery, false tax returns and false invoices, with its funds being used to fund a presidential re-election campaign and to make payments to the president's wife (invoiced as consulting services). Other non-arms examples include GSK (a UK drugs company) for bribing Chinese doctors and hospitals with cash and sexual favours, Balfour Beatty (UK) for construction contracts in Egypt, and Macmillan publishers (UK) for making payments to obtain orders in African states. Finally, Siemens AG (Germany) made payments to secure government contracts involving identity cards in Argentina, together with other government contracts for the construction of power plants, railway lines and medical equipment. Corruption has also been identified in sport (e.g., athletics, boxing, cricket, football, tennis).

The nations with the worst records for bribery and corruption include Angola, Afghanistan, Bangladesh, Brazil (e.g., Petrobras scandal), Iraq, Libya, North Korea, Somalia and South Sudan, with some of these countries having been involved in conflict (Transparency International 2015). Typically, bribery and corruption are associated with large rather than small firms.

A further aspect of non-price competition used by arms firms involves political lobbying. Arms firms often lobby governments, seeking to influence contract awards and the prices and profitability of contracts. For example, they might commission consultancy firms to undertake "independent" economic studies of major arms projects where they are bidding for the contract. Such studies will estimate the jobs, exports and industrial benefits of awarding the project to a national arms firm. While lobbying can seek to influence government procurement choices, it is not necessarily illegal; it might, however, be regarded as "unfair" if the lobbying process is not transparent. Typically, lobbying is a feature of any political system with individuals, groups, firms and industries seeking to influence government policy (e.g., smoking and the tobacco industry). Critics point to big business exercising undue influence on government, where big business embraces all industries and not only arms producers. Large firms form powerful producer interest groups that will seek to influence government policy (see Chapter 8). In democracies, lobbying is a feature of free speech and debate. Society has to decide whether any aspects of lobbying are regarded as "undesirable" and, if so, what the appropriate policy response should be. One possible response might be to create a public register of political lobby firms or of all lobbying activities, but such a response raises difficulties of definition, policing and monitoring.

There is a further aspect of non-price competition reflected in the labour market requirements of major arms producers. Firms seeking a competitive advantage in arms markets will hire ex-military staff and procurement officers to provide insider information and insider advantages (a policy known as "revolving doors"). Aerospace firms will hire retired air marshals, tank firms will hire ex-army generals, and warship producers will hire ex-admirals, all with the aim of obtaining information and knowledge and an insider advantage in competitions for arms contracts. Such recruitment policies are not usually illegal although some countries might require a suitable time gap between staff leaving the government service and being employed by an arms firm (or any other related firm). Nor are such recruitment practices unique to arms firms. Other industries pursue similar recruitment polices. Examples include pharmaceuticals, medical equipment suppliers, construction, transport and firms bidding for military outsourcing contracts.

The emergence of new markets: UAVs, cyber, terrorism, outsourcing

Arms markets are always changing, reflecting new technologies, new threats and new business prospects. Throughout history arms have changed: from swords to catapults, to bows and arrows, personal armour, trebuchet launchers and the use of horses, to cannons, castles and muskets. Until the early 1900s, warfare was fought only on land and at sea, with associated industries supplying, for example, cannons, muskets and warships. Following the first manned flight in 1903, air space was added to the domains of warfare. The years since have witnessed major changes in arms industries. New weapons include tanks and armoured fighting vehicles in the land domain; aircraft carriers and submarines in the sea dimension; and aircraft, helicopters, missiles, rockets and space systems in the aerospace domain. Surveillance and communications have advanced from flags to radio, radar and mobile phones. New weapons of mass destruction have emerged, embracing nuclear, chemical and biological weapons, with intercontinental rockets as the method of delivery. The result has been new arms producers and industries supplying aircraft, helicopters, missiles, rockets, satellites, submarines, tanks, armoured fighting vehicles and defence electronics. New methods of propulsion such as the jet engine, rocket motors and nuclear reactors (e.g., nuclear-powered submarines) have emerged.

By 2016, a number of new arms markets were emerging, including cyber and UAVs. Cyber security focuses on the protection of military and civil IT systems, including the protection of military communication systems (cyber warfare). UAVs (drones) are replacing manned combat aircraft for dangerous, high-risk military operations and for long-endurance surveillance tasks (e.g., maritime patrol). UAVs also provide spin-offs, with civil applications to policing, surveillance and mapping. These new markets affect arms industries through new entry and acquisitions. For example, new firms have emerged to supply UAVs, and established producers have also entered the UAV industry either through internal expansion (e.g., BAE Systems, Dassault Aviation) or through mergers and acquisitions.

Terrorism has created new markets and industries too. Terrorist threats have resulted in changing demands for arms from the armed forces (e.g., cyber security, including surveillance systems). Terrorism has also created new forms of arms industries based on individuals and small groups capable of developing and supplying small arms, home-made bombs, improvised explosive devices and human suicide bombers. Terrorist groups have also shown ingenuity in adapting civil products to military uses, such as small trucks converted into mobile light attack vehicles, and suicide bombers have provided both short- and long-range strike capabilities.

Another emerging arms market involves military outsourcing. This market involves private or state-owned firms undertaking activities traditionally supplied "in-house" by the armed forces. Examples include firms providing aircrew training, maintaining and repairing weapons, managing and maintaining military facilities, supplying transport and catering services, and supplying a range of other support activities (e.g., recovery of fighting vehicles from combat zones). Some examples of outsourcing are close to the front line, such as private firms providing air tanker operations for the air force (e.g., RAF air tankers being provided by a private contractor). Arms producers undertaking military outsourcing activities are involved in forward vertical integration, where the firm undertakes activities that use its outputs (e.g., an aircraft firm contracting to maintain and repair its aircraft). Outsourcing enables arms producers to enter new military markets that were previously protected from competition.

Some exceptions

There are exceptions to the account presented in this chapter involving small firms, arms dealers, illegal arms markets and mercenaries. Much of the focus on arms producers is on the major arms firms, which are large firms. However, some arms producers are small firms. These might be firms in the supply chain supplying parts and components to prime contractors. In addition, some producers of small arms are also small firms. For example, artisans produce basic firearms and they are widespread in West Africa, Pakistan and Colombia, where blacksmiths produce a range of small arms (e.g., pistols, assault rifles, mortars). In some cases, small arms are produced by terrorist and rebel groups (e.g., the IRA produced mortars, the Taliban has produced improvised explosive devices, and suicide bombers have been trained and supplied by terrorist groups (SAS 2015)).

The arms market is also facilitated and developed by arms dealers, who trade in a variety of arms, especially in small arms and parts. Arms dealers are individuals who specialize in arms trading, and their business is to bring together buyers and sellers of arms. However, this market trading function might sometimes involve illegal trading in the form of arms trafficking. As with all illegal activities, it is not possible to obtain reliable data on the illegal arms market. In contrast, legal arms trading, where the buyers are governments, is well documented (see Chapters 6 and 7).

One further dimension of arms trading is highly controversial and involves the use of mercenary forces: that is, private individuals and armies available for hire by foreign governments. Mercenary forces are a further source of demand for arms, mostly small arms, but as with arms dealers they are a relatively unknown dimension of the market. In contrast, much is known about private security companies, which are private firms providing security and guarding services. They are buyers of arms, mostly small arms, and they form part of the legal arms market.

Conclusion

The structure and conduct of arms producers is extraordinarily complex and departs from the simple and traditional economic analysis of industries. There are complex strategic interactions between small numbers of large arms firms and between large firms and governments. Large arms firms also form powerful producer groups that seek to influence governments, forming part of the military–industrial–political complex (see Chapter 8). Further complexity arises from illegal arms markets, where reliable data are unavailable. The public policy issues are clear. Arms producers involved in socially undesirable and/or illegal activities should be identified and subject to market failure analysis and policy or legal action. In the next chapter, we discuss the performance of arms producers. How well do they perform and do they provide "good value for money"?

Notes

1. There are examples where private markets have emerged to solve public goods problems. For example, traditional lighthouses provide free lighting and protection to all seafarers, but free-riding can be "solved" by replacing lighthouses with private monitoring and signalling devices that are purchased from the signalling station.
2. This claim reflects the fact that the US compares its defence burden (D/Y) with those of its European NATO allies. This comparison is misleading since the US defence burden reflects its defence of the US, Pacific and Mediterranean regions and Europe. In contrast, European NATO allies allocate most if not all of their defence spending to the defence of Europe.
3. This game is based on the behaviour of two individuals arrested for a crime where the police lack sufficient evidence to convict. The suspects are placed in separate cells and informed that the one who testifies against the other will be released; if neither confesses, both will be released; and if both confess, both will be imprisoned. The best outcome would be for both to remain silent, in which case both would be released; but this game shows that each suspect chooses an economically inefficient outcome, with both confessing, leading to both being imprisoned. A similar outcome arises where two firms make sealed bids for a contract.
4. Auctions might be used for the award of arms contracts. Auctions involve strategic behaviour by bidders and there is a considerable literature on the economics of various auction methods, including English and Dutch auctions and first- and second-price sealed bids. The "winner's curse" introduces the possibility that the winning bidder in a sealed bid auction might overbid (see Lipczynski *et al.* 2009).
5. One Boeing example concerned the USAF air tanker contract in 2003. A principal deputy under-secretary in the USAF was accused of using her position to award a favourable contract to Boeing and of disclosing to Boeing information on the rival Airbus bid: the official was subsequently employed by Boeing.

6

ARMS INDUSTRIES: PERFORMANCE

Introduction

Critics focus on arms producers being inefficient and operating in state-protected markets earning excessive profits at the expense of taxpayers. They point to a failure to manage major weapons projects, reflected in cost over-runs, delays and weapons that are costly and often fail to perform to their operational requirements. Further, it is claimed that any export successes are achieved either through large government subsidy payments or through the payments of bribes to foreign buyers, or both. Religious, moralist, ethical and peace groups also condemn arms industries for supplying products that kill and injure people.

Supporters of arms industries point to their military benefits in the form of supplying weapons that contribute to maintaining peace, protection and security for a nation's citizens, their property and their way of life. Contrary to the opponents of arms industries, some groups argue that arms producers save lives and protect a nation's citizens' independence and freedoms. There are additional wider economic benefits in the form of employment, technology, spin-offs, exports and import-savings benefits.

Are arms industries worthwhile industries?

How can these conflicting views be assessed? Economists need to assess the various arguments critically and consider the criteria for determining whether the arms industry is a worthwhile industry and one which should be retained. The economic criterion for a socially desirable change is demanding: namely, that change is desirable if one person can be made better off without making someone else worse off. In reality, this criterion is likely to be replaced by the less demanding criterion of cost–benefit analysis: do the benefits of change exceed the costs? But the fact that the issue of whether the arms industry is a worthwhile industry is being raised at all needs to be considered.

Typically, a competitive industry is regarded as worthwhile if consumers are willing to pay its economic price and the returns to the industry cover all its costs, earning at least normal profits. Here, profits are regarded as normal if they are sufficient to induce investors to remain in the industry, providing continued funding for the business. A failure to earn at least normal profits signals that there are more attractive alternative uses for investors' funds, which will therefore leave the industry and transfer to other uses.

Arms industries might be failing to work properly due to monopoly, externalities or public goods problems. But standard market analysis is inappropriate where there are no individual consumers of arms, where defence is a public good and the market is a political market. The dominant role of government means that questions about whether the arms industry is worth retaining are government choices. Admittedly, in democracies, voters can affect these choices, but voting systems are often limited mechanisms for reflecting voter preferences. For example, a system of general elections means that voter choices reflect a range of policy options (e.g., on income tax, public expenditure and welfare policies), with policy towards the national arms industry forming one component within the policy mix. A referendum system would allow voters to express preferences on specific issues (e.g., policy on a national arms industry), but referenda have their limitations as accurate indicators of all voter preferences (e.g., majority voting versus unanimity rules for reaching society's decisions). Voting systems are also limited in revealing society's true preferences for arms industries due to the public-goods and free-rider features of defence. Alternatively, in non-democratic systems, social choices are made by dictators, autocrats and unelected committees, reflecting *their* views and values on the national arms industry. Such views are not subject to democratic accountability.

Questions about whether the arms industry is worth retaining are not unique to the arms industry. Similar questions arise about industries such as the pharmaceutical, tobacco and alcohol industries, with critics pointing to their social undesirability (e.g., claims that smoking and drinking alcohol are harmful to health). However, other industries are not dependent on government demands. Instead, consumer demands and private firm behaviour can be changed by tax-subsidy policy, by state regulation and by state ownership. These policies can change industry output without eliminating the industry.

Performance indicators

An economic assessment of arms industries requires some indicators to assess their performance. In principle, a variety of indicators can be used, but in practice, published and reliable data are often lacking so alternative and limited published indicators have to be used. Examples of available indicators include data on cost escalation and delays on major arms projects, development timescales, output levels, firm size, productivity, unit costs, exports, imports and profitability. Ideally, similar data are required for foreign arms producers as well as civil industries to provide both national and international comparators. Comparisons with civil industries allow consideration of the opportunity cost question, namely, whether the resources currently allocated to arms industries would make a greater contribution to national output if they were used elsewhere in the economy; but the opportunity cost question requires that the alternative industries be identified. The rest of this chapter reviews examples of performance indicators for arms industries. The approach is meant to be illustrative rather than comprehensive. Project case studies are a useful starting point for an assessment of industry performance.

Project case studies

Eleven combat aircraft projects – comprising aircraft from Europe, the US, Russia and Japan – are taken to illustrate the case study approach. The projects are the European Gripen, Rafale and Typhoon aircraft; the US F-15,

F-16, F-18E/F, F-22 and F-35 combat aircraft; the Russian MiG-29 and Su-27; and the Japanese F-2. The case study data are presented in Table 6.1.

Table 6.1 Project case studies: combat aircraft, 2015.

Project	Prime contractor	Dev. time (months)	Output (units)	Exports (units)	Productivity ($000s per employee)	Profitability (%)
Gripen	Saab	207	287	111	222,153	7.0
Rafale	Dassault	224	370	84	398,212	8.6
Typhoon	Eurofighter	243	599	127	365,247	6.3
F-15E Strike Eagle	Boeing	85	528	315	595,502	8.1
F-16	Lockheed Martin	79	4,588	2,344	366,127	11.9
F-18E/F	Boeing	84	737	36	595,502	8.1
F-22 Raptor	Lockheed Martin	78	195	0	366,127	11.9
F-35 Lightning	Lockheed Martin	224	3,178	721	366,127	11.9
MiG-29	Mikoyan	106	1,625	660	52,800	13.0
Su-27	Sukhoi	132	870	337	52,800	13.0
F-2	Mitsubishi Heavy Industries	128	98	0	539,893	5.3

Notes. (i) Output and export numbers in unit volumes are approximations: some are security sensitive (e.g., Russian aircraft), others include options, some include different variants (e.g., Gripen includes an E version). Total output includes exports. Data are for 2015/16. (ii) Development times are in months and are from start date to in-service date. Some aircraft were developments of existing aircraft (e.g., F-15, F-18E/F), giving the appearance of short development times. (iii) In-service dates are November 1997 for Gripen, May 2001 for Rafale, August 2003 for Typhoon, January 1976 for F-15E, August 1978 for F-16, February 2000 for F-18E/F, December 2005 for F-22, July 2015 for F-35 (B variant), July 1982 for MiG-29, June 1985 for Su-27, and June 2000 for F-2. The definition of in-service dates can vary; also, where the month was not published, it was assumed to be mid-year (i.e. June). (iv) Productivity and profitability figures are for total company business, comprising military and civil sales, in 2015. For example, Boeing sales, productivity and profitability are based on its total business, including sales of civil aircraft. Profits are percentage returns on sales for 2015. Data for the Typhoon are median figures from Airbus, BAE and Finmeccanica/Leonardo.

Assembling project case study data is not without problems. For example, identifying the start date of a project can be difficult: the start might be the earliest recorded date of work on the aircraft or the formal award of a contract. Similarly, the in-service date might be the date of first delivery to the services or the date of initial operating capability. The definition of initial operating capability can differ over time and between nations, and the first date for in-service delivery might embrace different definitions of the operational performance of first deliveries (e.g., early deliveries might not have a full weapons fit, they might lack radar, or they might have an early version of the jet engine).

Development times are a performance indicator but with limitations. Development times need to be accompanied by development cost data, recognizing that faster development might be costly. Output data also have their limitations. For example, output and export totals might not be based on identical definitions, with some totals including planned orders as well as actual deliveries. Export totals also have their limitations as a performance indicator since governments might prevent the overseas sales of some aircraft (e.g., F-22) or impose restrictions on the quality of export sales (e.g., sales of Apache attack helicopters without Longbow radar; US restrictions on the export of armed UAVs).

The data in Table 6.1 lead us to four broad conclusions. First, US combat aircraft have the shortest (fastest) development times (except for the F-35). However, the existence of a development cost–time trade-off suggests that the faster US timescales might be achieved at higher cost. Second, the collaborative Typhoon project had the longest development time, raising questions about whether collaboration caused such lengthy development. Third, the development time and exports sales for the Gripen and Rafale show that European national programmes can be as competitive as collaboration. Fourth, using export *volume* totals as an indicator of competitiveness, we find that the US F-16 and F-35 and the Russian MiG-29 aircraft are the most successful in the sample (the F-35 figures are based on *projected* output and exports and not actual totals). Admittedly, volume data differ from export value data, but export values are notoriously difficult to obtain and are sensitive to the export package (e.g., whether it is for acquisition only or includes support, weapons, spares and training for varying numbers of years as well as offsets).

Labour productivity and profitability are further performance indicators but each has major limitations. Table 6.1 shows substantial variations in productivity between the extremes of Boeing and Mikoyan/Sukhoi. But problems arise in ensuring internationally standard definitions of productivity and in recognizing that different productivity figures reflect different degrees of firm vertical integration (i.e. different degrees of buying-in parts and components); it needs to also be noted that the data in Table 6.1 are based on total company operations comprising *all* military and civil sales. For example, the high productivity figures for Boeing reflect its large-scale production of civil aircraft (leading to economies of scale and learning, resulting in higher productivity). A more accurate productivity indicator needs to be based on value-added productivity, which ideally needs to be shown for a firm's arms sales only.

Problems also arise with profitability data, which reflect all military and civil sales and do not reflect the actual profitability on each of the project case studies. Nonetheless, comparisons with US, European, Japanese and global data for aerospace and defence, motor vehicles and all industries provided no evidence of "excessive" profits being earned by the defence firms listed in Table 6.1.[1] However, the data in Table 6.1 should be regarded as suggestive rather than comprehensive and conclusive. There are two major omissions from the table: namely, a lack of data on both the unit costs of each aircraft and their operational performance.

Table 6.2 presents data on unit flyaway costs and operational performance for a sample of modern combat aircraft. Again, the data are based on published sources only and are presented as an illustration of the approach; they are not meant to be accurate and comprehensive. Typically, greater performance in terms of effectiveness is costlier, with greater performance bought at greater cost. The F-22 is a very effective combat aircraft, but it is costly. Similarly, the European national projects – namely, the Gripen and Rafale – are lower cost than the collaborative Typhoon, but they are less effective. Also, there is a trade-off between quality and quantity (e.g., about four F-16s for one F-22). The F-16 is relatively cheap but it is considerably less effective than the F-22. However, while unit cost figures are often available in the public domain, data on operational performance are much more difficult to obtain. Even unit cost data can be misleading indicators of total costs, and care is needed to identify the true costs of arms. For example, unit flyaway costs are unit production or recurring unit costs for aircraft. They comprise all direct and indirect manufacturing costs and their associated overheads, but they form only one component of total unit costs. Unit acquisition costs comprise R & D as well as unit flyaway costs, but even these are only partial indicators of the total unit costs of arms. Further costs involving maintenance and support arise over a weapon's life cycle, resulting in life cycle costs. The quantity of aircraft that are purchased also affects unit cost and total costs, so costs are not a simple concept!

Table 6.2   Cost and performance data for combat aircraft.

Aircraft	Unit flyaway cost ($ millions, 2013 prices)	Effectiveness score
F-22	273	0.9
F-35A	184	NA
Typhoon	138	0.75
F-15E	126	0.55
Rafale M	100	0.5
F18E/F	61	0.45
Gripen C	53	0.4
F-16C	70	0.21

Notes. (i) Cost data for F-15E based on F-15C. Rafale and Gripen prices include VAT. (ii) Higher effectiveness scores show a greater probability that the fighter will win a combat based on beyond visual range air-to-air combat, based on a UK study of 1994. (iii) NA denotes "not available".
Source: Defence Committee (1992) and Lorrell (1995).

Further performance indicators in the form of cost overruns and delays are also used to assess the efficiency of arms industries. Here, definitions are needed to distinguish cost overruns from cost escalation. Overruns, or cost growth, occur where the costs of a project rise above their original estimates (ideally all expressed in constant prices for the same project). Escalation arises where costs increase between successive generations of equipment (e.g., the unit cost of a Typhoon is higher than that of the previous-generation Tornado aircraft).

Cost overruns and delays

Critics of arms industries claim that their inefficiencies are reflected in cost overruns, delays and costly weapons, and there is certainly evidence supporting such claims. Nations with a substantial arms industry supply high-technology weapons, which are costly and are characterized by cost increases and slippages in delivery, and which often fail to work properly. Table 6.3 presents some UK and US evidence. For example, UK aircraft carriers and attack submarines are costly and both have shown substantial cost increases and delays in delivery (e.g., an almost five-year delay for Astute submarines). Carriers are even costlier when their aircraft are included in the cost figures. But, by itself, evidence of costly weapons, cost overruns and delays could be consistent with arms producers being either technically efficient or inefficient! With only this evidence, both interpretations are plausible; more careful analysis and evidence is required to reach a definitive conclusion.

Cost increases might lead to the cancellation of arms projects. Two examples occurred in the UK: namely, the TSR-2 strike aircraft, which was cancelled in April 1965; and the Nimrod MRA4 maritime patrol aircraft, which was cancelled in 2010. Rising unit costs and the lower costs of a US alternative, namely, the F-111, led to the cancellation of TSR-2. At the time of cancellation, the unit costs of TSR-2 were some £5.8 million, compared with an estimated unit cost of the US F-111 of £2.125 million. However, further development of the F-111 led to rising costs, and by September 1967 the unit price of the F-111 had risen to £2.95 million, which was still much cheaper than the cancelled TSR-2. In addition, the US agreed to an offset package providing work for UK industry. Events changed and in early 1968, in response to an earlier devaluation and cuts in public spending with defence bearing its "fair share", the UK announced the cancellation of its order for the F-111 (Moore 2015).

The Nimrod MRA4 was cancelled as part of the UK's 2010 Strategic Defence Review. The project started in 1996 with an order for 21 aircraft at an estimated cost of £2.8 billion. At the time of cancellation, the aircraft had cost £3.4 billion, the project was running over nine years late, it was £789 million over budget, its unit costs were three times the figure expected at the start of the project, procurement numbers had declined to nine aircraft, and it was still subject to operational shortfalls. Cancellation was expected to lead to cost savings of almost £2 billion. The official causes of cancellation included industry underestimating the design challenges, weak programme management, poor forecasting, and Ministry of Defence budget problems (NAO 2011).

Table 6.3 Cost overruns and delays: UK and US.

Total expected cost to completion at start of project (£ millions)	Current 2015 forecast cost to completion (£ millions)
UK equipment projects	
All 13 largest UK projects: 60,281	65,833 (9.2% cost increase)
Examples	
Queen Elizabeth aircraft carriers: 3,541	6,212 (75% cost increase)
Typhoon combat aircraft: 15,173	17,341 (14% cost increase)
Astute attack submarines: Boats 1–3: 2,233	3,536 (58% cost increase)
A400M airlifter: 2,238	2,710 (21% cost increase)
Delays on 12 projects:	+60 months
US major defence projects	US cost growth (%)
Army	2.1
Navy	7.4
Air Force	3.8
US Totals	4.6

Notes. (i) UK cost data based on 13 largest UK equipment projects. Delays are additional delays based on 12 largest UK equipment projects. (ii) US cost growth is shown separately for each service and for all US major projects. Cost growth is for base year to December 2015 based on "then" year dollars and it includes all price or cost increases expected over the duration of the programme.
Sources: NAO (2015) and US DoD (2015).

Cost overruns on arms projects are not confined to Western-type capitalist economies. China's defence industry has shown major weaknesses. Its arms industry has six sectors dominated by state-owned firms with no outside competition. A US Rand study identified a list of weaknesses reflected in delays, cost overruns and quality control problems. Further weaknesses of China's defence industry included corruption, a lack of competition and entrenched monopolies, bureaucratic fragmentation, an outdated acquisition system, and restricted access to external sources of technology and expertise (Chase *et al* 2015).

Other countries have also cancelled arms projects, for a variety of different reasons. The US cancelled a number of military projects, including the Future Combat System, the Comanche attack helicopter, the airborne laser and the Presidential helicopter. Russia cancelled the MiG Skat (flying wing) and Su-47 aircraft (Berkut: forward swept wing), France cancelled its Mirage 4000 fighter aircraft, Canada cancelled its Avro Canada Arrow fighter aircraft in 1959, and Israel cancelled its Lavi fighter aircraft in 1987.

To understand costly weapons, cost overruns and delays, one needs a model that shows the determinants of these outcomes. Costly weapons reflect the demands from the armed forces for the latest high-technology equipment. Weapons as tournament goods will always be costly as each military service seeks equipment capable of meeting all possible military threats from potential enemies (attaining a winning margin). Economic models of cost overruns and delays suggest that a given level of equipment performance can be achieved with various combinations of development cost and time: trade-offs show that shorter timescales are costlier, leading to cost overruns. Military requirements for higher performance can lead to both higher costs and longer timescales, reflected in cost overruns and delays. Furthermore, cost overruns arise where the military and defence ministries change their original preferences and require equipment "urgently": faster development is costlier. At this point, arms producers are passive agents reacting to the demands of the armed forces and the constraints of technology (including behavioural factors and optimism bias in procurement agencies (Bangert & Davies 2015)). However, arms producers might have a more active role where they deliberately bid a low price in an effort to win a major arms contract. Such behaviour can arise where governments award cost-plus or cost-based contracts to a successful bidder, where such contracts fail to provide "hard" budget constraints. The pricing situation is complicated further when arms producers operate in non-competitive markets, where their price bids are not subject to competition from rivals and where an arms producer might be a "national champion" that might be "too big to fail" (a moral hazard problem). With cost-based contracts and non-competitive markets, a contractor's rising costs can be shifted to taxpayers, which is where contractor inefficiencies arise (Hartley 2011a: 111). In such circumstances, the challenge for defence ministries is to negotiate prices and profits that minimize contractor inefficiency (see Chapter 7). Various nations have attempted to control cost growth and delays through reforms in defence procurement but often with little success and the phenomenon continues. The ultimate sanction on cost overruns and delays is the cancellation of a project, leading to further accusations of "waste and inefficiency" both in government and in the arms industries.

Cost overruns and delays have both military and industrial impacts. Defence ministries and the armed forces have to take responsibility for managing costs and reducing optimism bias; they have to recognize that trade-offs between cost, time and performance might require sacrifices in performance; some national military capabilities might have to be sacrificed; and nations need to be more willing to buy off the shelf, especially from overseas. There are also industrial feedback effects. Higher unit costs result in smaller numbers being procured and a loss of learning and scale economies, which in turn leads to incentives for industrial consolidation (acquisitions and mergers). But high costs, overruns and delays are not necessarily undesirable. They might lead to socially beneficial improvements in equipment, resulting in cost-effective weapons systems that contribute to peace and security (where the benefits of equipment modifications are valued more highly than the extra costs).

In assessing the performance of arms producers using cost overruns and delays, comparisons are needed with other industries: what is the experience of non-defence industries? Typically, cost overruns and delays are not uniquely confined to arms producers: they arise in other public sector projects embracing construction, energy and transportation. US studies show typical cost overruns of 50 per cent to 100 per cent in real terms for large projects. Examples include the construction of canals, dams and hospitals, the costs of cleaning up nuclear weapons sites, creating urban rail systems, and the construction of sites for the Olympic Games (Edwards & Kaeding 2015). Other large public sector projects showing substantial cost overruns include the Sydney Opera House (14 times over budget and ten years late), the Scottish Parliament Building (ten times cost increase) and the construction of major international airports.

Various causes have been offered for cost overruns including modifications, unexpected problems and unexpected increases in the prices of factor inputs, as well as optimism bias by project planners. In some cases, cost overruns might not be presented on a consistent and constant price basis and might be an amalgam of different price indices or of current price data from different years. Interestingly, across a sample of projects, it should be expected that cost estimating errors would show under-budgeting as well as cost overruns, but the reality is different, and projects generally run over budget and not under budget. Such results reflect behaviour and incentives in political markets: there are incentives to start a major project by submitting initially low cost estimates and optimistic estimates of benefits, and once started major projects are difficult to stop (see Chapter 8).

Nor are cost overruns and delays confined to public sector projects. Private sector projects displaying such characteristics include the Airbus A380 and Boeing 787 airliners, IT projects and R & D costs for new pharmaceutical products. However, cost overruns and delays on private sector projects are financed by private investors rather than taxpayers, and those responsible for such outcomes are subject to penalties in the form of job losses, takeovers and bankruptcy.

Defence inflation and cost escalation

Defence inflation and cost escalation are a source of rising costs in defence budgets. Defence-specific inflation consists of rising prices for defence goods and services: it affects the prices of all factor inputs into money defence spending. Often, defence inflation exceeds the economy's general rate of inflation as measured by the GDP deflator. Defence inflation contributes to the rising costs of both equipment and military personnel inputs (capital and labour) into the defence production process. The causes of defence inflation need to be identified, with a starting point being any distinctive features of arms markets.

Cost escalation differs from defence inflation. It focuses on the rising real unit costs between successive generations of new equipment (e.g., Tornado to Typhoon combat aircraft). Defence inflation contributes to intergeneration cost escalation in money terms. Both contribute to cost overruns on arms projects (Hartley & Solomon 2016).

Performance: tariffs, subsidies and corruption

Not all aspects of arms industry performance show efficient behaviour based on price competition reflecting least-cost production. Performance might reflect government preferential purchasing from national champions. Or performance might reflect tariff protection and the payment of subsidies to arms producers. Tariffs protect domestic arms firms from foreign competition, and subsidies provide firms with cost advantages. There is also the possibility that some aspects of arms industry performance might be subject to, and the result of, bribery and corruption.

Contract awards are obvious targets for bribery and corruption. Arms producers have incentives to use bribes to influence contract awards. Examples of bribery allegations and proven cases have involved arms firms in France, Germany, Italy, South Africa, the UK and the US. Thales (France) was fined for bribes in its 1991 sale of frigates to Taiwan; Leonardo (Italy) was banned from bidding for Indian defence contracts; and German defence contractors were accused of offering bribes for the award of Greek defence contracts (tanks and submarines). Bribery takes many forms, involving cash payments and payments-in-kind such as air travel, expensive clothing, hotel accommodation, sexual favours and gifts of expensive motor cars. As a result, the export performance of arms producers might reflect bribery and corruption rather than efficiency.

Conclusion

Any critique of arms industries needs an understanding of causal factors derived from economic models. All too often, the temptation is to rely on unsubstantiated claims and assertions that reflect value judgements. Such claims need to be identified, exposed and assessed critically. The underlying market conditions and firm behaviour need to be addressed. Claims also need to be tested against the available evidence, which in many instances is not available in the public domain (e.g., evidence on the combat-effectiveness of weapons systems). The next two chapters provide more insights into buying arms and the implications of the military–industrial–political complex.

Notes

1. In January 2016 profit sales ratios for US aerospace and defence industries were 14.4 per cent; the corresponding figure for Europe was 10.6 per cent; for Japan it was 9.7 per cent; and the global figure was 12.7 per cent. Similarly, profit rates for all US industry were 16.3 per cent; for European industry the figure was 13.7 per cent; for all Japanese industry it was 9.8 per cent; and the corresponding global figure was 14.1 per cent in 2016 (Damodoran 2016).

7

BUYING ARMS

Introduction

Buying arms appears to be a simple process: the armed forces decide on their requirements and buy from arms producers who meet their requirements at the lowest price. Reality is different, and buying arms is a much more complex process. It is not like buying a car, television or mobile phone, all of which exist and can be sampled before buying. Armed forces often require weapons that do not yet exist and have to be "tailor made" for the military. Also, governments usually interfere with armed forces procurement choices as they pursue military–strategic interests and wider economic benefits by buying arms from national suppliers. These claimed military and wider economic benefits need to be assessed critically and costed. For example, buying from national arms producers can be costly and risky compared with purchasing existing arms "off the shelf" from overseas suppliers. This chapter assesses the arguments.

Buying arms is a complex process

Arms buying involves choices about what to buy, who to buy from, how to buy and when to buy.

What to buy?

The armed forces and governments have to decide the type of equipment needed. This requires an assessment of future threats and the available budget, where both threats and budgets are characterized by uncertainty. Moreover, uncertainty is increased where the arms required do not yet exist and have to be developed and produced for a specific national requirement. Here, the armed forces have to specify the operational performance of the weapons they need (e.g., speed and range of combat aircraft, firepower of tanks), which might involve major technical advances, further increasing uncertainty. Technical change might render current arms obsolescent. Examples include the development of ballistic rockets replacing long-range strategic bombers, nuclear weapons replacing large-scale conventional forces, jet engines replacing propeller aircraft, and UAVs replacing manned aircraft. Further complications arise where governments interfere with arms procurement choices for military–strategic interests and wider economic benefits.

Who to buy from: choice of contractor?

Once a requirement has been formulated, a contractor has to be selected, either using competition or direct negotiation with a preferred supplier. Competition can be restricted to domestic arms producers or extended to include foreign firms. Much depends on whether existing arms are purchased or whether completely new weapons are required. Developing and producing a completely new weapon further increases costs and the risks of failure compared with buying existing arms off the shelf.

How to buy: choice of contract?

Once a contractor has been selected, the type of contract has to be determined. Contract types vary from fixed price to cost-plus, each with different efficiency and incentive properties. Fixed-price contracts provide a fixed lump sum payment that, in principle, remains unchanged regardless of the contractor's actual costs: hence, if costs rise above their estimated level, all the cost overruns are borne by the firm, and similarly, if costs are below the estimated level, the firm retains all of the difference between estimated and actual costs. As a result, fixed-price contracts provide "high-powered" incentives. An example is the USAF fixed-price development contract for the new Boeing KC46A Pegasus tanker aircraft (valued at $5.85 billion), which in 2016 was reported to have cost Boeing some $1.9 billion in cost overruns and is subject to delays (Trimble 2016a). These cost overruns and delays have arisen from a new tanker aircraft that is based on an established design (Boeing 767). The opposite extreme is a cost-plus contract, which refunds the contractor's costs whatever their level plus a percentage profit rate based on actual costs. Such contracts have been termed "blank cheque" contracts and provide no efficiency incentives. Between the extremes of fixed-price and cost-plus contracts, there are various types of target cost incentive contracts, where the risks of cost overruns and any underruns are shared between the government and the contractor, with or without a maximum price limit.

When to buy?

This choice has various dimensions involving competition over a project's life cycle. At one extreme, where a completely new weapon is required, the armed forces will have to select from drawing board designs with the possibility of a "paper competition" between rival designs; or they might promote a prototype competition before making a final selection. For example, the US Joint Strike Fighter selection was based on a competition between two prototypes from Boeing and Lockheed Martin (a fly-off), with Lockheed Martin winning the competition to develop and supply the F-35 Lightning II aircraft. Once this contract was awarded, Lockheed Martin became a monopoly supplier. Alternatively, the armed forces could complete the development of a weapon and introduce competition for the production contract. Or, a weapon might be purchased off the shelf from a firm that has already developed and produced the equipment. For example, a number of nations are buying the US F-35 combat aircraft from Lockheed Martin although there is competition from suppliers of rival aircraft (e.g., F-15, F-18, Gripen, Rafale, Typhoon). A further possibility would extend competition into the refurbishing stage of the life cycle (e.g., by inviting competition for refurbishing and upgrading a weapon). These various options allow rivalry to be introduced into a monopoly supplier position.

Costs and risks

Modern high-technology arms such as nuclear-powered submarines, aircraft carriers, warships, combat aircraft and complex missiles are both costly and risky. Costs reflect risks. High-risk projects incur costs to solve their technical problems in ensuring that the weapons actually perform as required by the armed forces; also, the armed forces can change their requirements over time, adding further to costs and to timescales. Economists focus on marginal changes, and beyond a certain level of technology, further increases in performance become increasingly costly.

There are various myths about costs, some of which arise from focusing on one component of costs, rather than on life-cycle costs, and ignoring "hidden costs". Compared with buying arms off the shelf from foreign suppliers, especially US firms, buying arms from national suppliers appears costly. Volume is an important determinant of unit costs and prices, and US arms firms derive economic benefits from their large home market, providing economies of scale and learning leading to competitive prices. Critics of buying arms from small-scale national producers claim that their unit prices are high and that national development programmes are prone to cost overruns and delays. However, foreign firms, including US firms, cannot avoid cost overruns and delays, and cost overruns can be shifted partly to foreign buyers of arms: much depends on whether the government of the supplying nation will be willing to waive an R & D levy on foreign sales and the subsequent pricing of spares, maintenance and modification work. It is not unknown for foreign arms to appear to be cheap when it comes to acquisition but expensive when it comes to paying for spares and modifications!

Importing foreign arms also means that the importing nation becomes dependent on foreign sources of supply and resupply in any conflict, where the foreign nation can impose an arms embargo and prevent arms being supplied. Arms embargoes have reputation effects for foreign suppliers, meaning that foreign arms firms might be regarded as "unreliable" in any future conflict. In other words, a proper economic evaluation of foreign purchases compared with buying from a national arms producer needs to include wider and "hidden" costs and benefits, involving independence, resupply in conflict, arms designed for the requirements of national armed forces, and the wider economic benefits of national purchasing. All too often the comparison between national and foreign purchases of arms focuses on one easily observed component of cost: namely, the initial acquisition price. It might also be the case that the comparison is based on the initial estimated unit cost at an early stage in project development, where such estimates are unreliable. Furthermore, foreign exchange rates can vary over time, adding an additional dimension to the risks of buying from abroad (there are mechanisms for some limited protection against currency fluctuations).

Nations often adopt policies to reduce the costs and risks of buying arms. Consider a nation that buys from national arms producers. Buying a completely new weapon involves risks of failure (the equipment might not work). Such risks of failure can be reduced by developing two or more alternative projects, providing insurance against one project failing and providing a competitive stimulus to the development teams.[1] The UK in the 1950s used duplicate aircraft development programmes to provide insurance against risks of project failure. For example, in the early 1950s, it developed two similar types of fighter aircraft: the Hawker Hunter and the Supermarine Swift. In the event, the Swift failed to perform as a fighter aircraft and was cancelled for that role, being replaced by the Hunter. Similarly, the UK developed three types of V-bomber, each providing insurance against one of the others failing. In the event, it was decided that each of the three types would be purchased (the Valiant, Victor and Vulcan; after ten years in service, though, the Valiant was retired prematurely due to unexpected fatigue problems).

Duplicate development is costlier than single-source development so nations often prefer the latter, leading to a monopoly for the selected developer; however, the expected cost savings might not be fully realized. A single developer is a monopoly whose costs might not be as low as under duplicate development, where there is a competitive stimulus;[2] additionally, possible cost savings from selecting a single developer might increase the risks of project failure. In reality, various policy options are available to reduce arms costs.

Reducing arms costs: the options

Arms can be purchased in various ways ranging from buying nationally to importing, with a range of intermediate options. Buying from national arms producers provides military–strategic and wider economic benefits. National arms industries can provide independence and security of resupply in conflict, and the weapons can be defined to meet the specific and special requirements of the nation's armed forces. National arms purchases also provide wider economic benefits in the form of jobs, technology, spin-offs, exports and import-savings. But national independence can be costly in both development and production costs. Buying nationally requires the government to fund all the development costs of the project, and unit production costs might be high due to small-scale production based on small national orders, which, in turn, will have to bear the fixed development costs that determine total unit costs.

At the opposite extreme to national purchasing is importing an existing weapon from an overseas supplier. In principle, foreign purchases mean that the importing nation only contributes a proportion of total development costs and will further benefit from the economies of scale and learning associated with buying from a large-scale producer. US arms firms are the classic example, with state funding of advanced-technology arms and large-scale production for the US home market (e.g., US planned orders for some 2,400 F-35 aircraft). Furthermore, foreign purchases mean that the weapons exist and have been in operational service so there are no risks of project failure (they can be tested before purchase). It is also possible for a foreign buyer to require equipment modifications to meet national requirements, although such modifications come at a cost. For example, the UK purchase of US Phantom aircraft (1964–6) involved UK inputs of avionics and Rolls-Royce engines, which led to higher unit costs, with the unit price of the UK Phantoms being some three times higher than that of US Phantoms. Similarly, the UK purchase of Boeing Apache helicopters in 1995 involved UK avionics and Rolls-Royce engines with final assembly at the AgustaWestland plant in the UK. More recently, the 2016 buy of 50 new Apache helicopters at a total price of $2.3 billion involved a direct purchase from Boeing with some sub-contract work for UK firms. A competitive threat from Leonardo led Boeing to offer an "attractive" price to win the contract, and an off-the-shelf buy allowed the UK to benefit from US economies of scale.

Between the extremes of national and foreign purchases of arms, there are intermediate policy options involving licensed production and international collaboration. A nation might achieve some of the wider military and economic benefits through the licensed production of an existing foreign weapon (e.g., aircraft, tanks, warships). Or, a nation might develop and produce arms on an international collaborative basis, where two or more nations share development costs and combine their production orders. Or, exports enable a national arms producer to achieve a larger-scale output, with the associated economies of scale and learning and contributions to retaining a national defence industry with its associated military–strategic and wider economic benefits. Arms export markets are competitive, with large oligopoly firms bidding for contracts (e.g., US and European firms). Inevitably, competition leads to lower prices and offers of attractive industrial packages comprising work shares and technology transfers.

All equipment procurement options offer various combinations of price, wider benefits and cost penalties. For example, work share is often a factor in the procurement choice. At its simplest, a national purchase provides maximum work share for the domestic economy whereas a foreign purchase means that the exporting nation obtains all the work share. Table 7.1 presents an information matrix showing the benefits and costs of alternative arms procurement policies. The numbers are illustrative examples and should be regarded as orders of magnitude only: they are based on comparisons with a national buy. For example, compared with a national buy, a foreign purchase might require a 10 per cent contribution to total development costs, unit production costs might be much less than 90 per cent of those for a national buy, and a foreign buy provides no work share and no military–strategic benefits. In contrast, compared with a national buy, international collaboration between two nations with equal sharing means that each contributes to 50 per cent of total development costs, there is a saving of 10 per cent in unit production costs, and each nation achieves an equal share of work and military–strategic benefits. Finally, licensed production might require a 10 per cent contribution to total development costs, unit production costs are likely to be identical to those for a national buy, and there might be a 5–10 per cent share of work and military–strategic benefits.

Table 7.1   Arms procurement options.

Option	Total development cost	Unit production cost	Work share	Military–strategic benefits
National buy	100%	100%	100%	100%
Licensed production	10%	100%	5–10%	5–10%
International collaboration	50%	90%	50%	50%
Foreign purchase	10%	<90%	0%	0%

Notes. (i) The baseline comparison is with the national buy and assumes a single and common cost curve for each option. (ii) International collaboration is based on a two-nation equal partnership with equal sharing of development costs and pooling of their equal production orders.

Of course, Table 7.1 does not show the key element in any procurement choice: namely, the features of the equipment in each policy option. Equipment features embrace such factors as operational performance, delivery dates and numbers. Complications arise here, since each option typically involves different types of equipment that are not perfect substitutes, so choices involve trade-offs. Nor are all policy options presented. Modifications and variants exist, which affects work share. For example, a foreign purchase might involve offsets where the buying nation receives some work share either directly on the imported military equipment or on other military equipment or on civil projects (e.g., aid for tourism). Similarly, an alternative to licensed production is some form of co-production, where two or more nations share the total production work. Some of these procurement options are explored below.

Offsets

Offsets are a feature of the arms trade, especially for aerospace equipment. Offsets are an agreement by an arms exporter to place some work in the buying nation, thereby relocating work from the supplying country to the buying nation. This relocation resembles trade diversion, which economists criticize as inefficient and welfare-reducing.

Offsets are direct or indirect. *Direct* offsets involve the buying nation's industry participating in some aspect of the contract for supplying foreign arms. For example, firms in the buying nation might be allocated work on parts and components for the imported arms. *Indirect* offsets allocate work to the importing nation either on some other military equipment or on a civil project. Unsurprisingly, offsets are dominated by myths, emotion and special pleading. When bidding for foreign arms contracts, firms have incentives to offer attractive offset packages, and they will seek new and ingenious methods of meeting their contractual requirements. For example, banks might offer arms firms attractive offset packages consisting of a bundle of overseas sales that can be claimed as offsets to meet the contractual requirements. Banks can also help a foreign arms supplier to achieve its offset targets. Or, flights by an arms producer's staff on foreign airlines might qualify as part of an offset. Here, the key question in assessing offsets is whether they represent genuinely new business that would not have been obtained without the offset agreement. For example, the UK purchase of the Boeing airborne warning aircraft (AWACS) involved offsets of 130 per cent of the value of the contract, but the offset included the sales of Rolls-Royce engines on civil aircraft that would have been obtained without the offset (House of Commons 1989). Estimates show that genuinely new business might be 25–50 per cent of the total offset.

Offsets might not be inefficient. They might contribute to efficiency improvements if they discover lower-cost overseas suppliers in the buying nation. Even so, further reservations remain. Offsets might involve higher costs for the buying nation as it seeks to discover firms able to undertake offset work to the standard required by the foreign arms supplier. Claims that offsets involve high-technology work need to be assessed critically. For advanced-technology arms, the technological problems will have been solved in the development stage: hence, claims that offsets involve advanced-technology work are misleading and exaggerated. For example, on the UK purchase of the Boeing AWACS, work on aircraft galleys including toilets was counted as high technology! Also, indirect offsets for civil work do not contribute to maintaining or developing a national arms industry. An alternative buying option involves co-production.

Licensed production and co-production

Co-production is a variant of licensed production that involves the buying nation sharing in total production work. Licensed production involves a foreign government or firm purchasing a licence allowing it to produce foreign-designed arms. Typically, licensed production involves the final assembly of foreign-designed military equipment (e.g., combat or trainer aircraft). In contrast, co-production involves both the supplying and buying nations sharing their total production work. A classic example was the decision by a consortium of four European nations to buy the US F-16 aircraft jointly, on a co-production contract (1975). Under this contract, the four-nation European consortium was awarded production work based on a 10 per cent share of the initial US order (650 aircraft) plus 40 per cent of the European order (348 aircraft) and a further 15 per cent of export sales to other countries. Belgium and the Netherlands were involved in the final assembly of F-16s for the Europeans, while Belgium supplied the engines and radar. There were other political–military benefits, including demonstrating support for the NATO alliance. However, co-production involved cost penalties of 34 per cent on unit costs for the Europeans compared with buying directly from General Dynamics, USA (later acquired by Lockheed Martin (see Rich *et al* 1981)).

Co-production further illustrates the options created by arms firms to obtain export sales. Other examples have included offsets, industrial collaboration, work sharing and technology transfer. More recently, co-development, which involves two or more nations sharing development costs on an agreed basis, has emerged as another option. For example, the UK is a co-developer on the US F-35 Lightning II aircraft, contributing 10 per cent of the estimated development cost and receiving a 15 per cent share of work on each F-35 produced (e.g., for BAE, Rolls-Royce, Cobham, GE Aviation and Martin Baker). A more complex policy option for cost and work sharing involves international collaboration.

International collaboration

International collaboration involves two or more nations developing and producing arms equipment. There has been extensive experience of such collaboration in Europe embracing aerospace projects. Examples include the Typhoon and Tornado combat aircraft, the A400M airlifter, the NH90 and Merlin helicopters, and a range of missile systems. Such projects have at least four distinguishing characteristics. First, they involved European nations only (France, Germany, Italy, Spain and the UK). Second, they involved the sharing of development as well as production work. This contrasts with some collaborative NATO projects, where a US company takes design leadership and the production work is shared (e.g., the NATO Sea Sparrow missile project). Third, they have involved various European nations in different collaborations, often with different organizational arrangements. Fourth, they have mostly been restricted to aerospace projects, embracing both military and civil aerospace projects (e.g., Airbus, the European Space Agency). There has been limited experience with European collaboration for land and sea systems.

Some examples of aerospace collaboration have involved European and non-European nations. For example, the AV-8B, or Harrier II, was a UK–US collaboration on the development of the UK-designed Harrier combat aircraft (an example of the US collaborating on the development of a foreign technology; an in-service date of 1985). Similarly, the AMX combat aircraft was the result of a collaboration between Italy and Brazil: this collaboration involved no duplication of work (an in-service date of 1989).

International collaboration involves complex choices, requiring different nations to agree their arms requirements and negotiate work shares, especially the allocation of the high-technology work between partner nations and their national champions. Typically, work shares are based on the size of each nation's production orders. The economics of international collaboration are appealing. Consider the simple case of two nations with equal sharing compared with each nation undertaking a national programme. In the ideal case, two equal partner nations on an aircraft project would share R & D costs equally and a doubling of output would lead to economies of scale and learning, resulting in lower unit production costs, probably of some 5–10 per cent.

But reality is different, with international collaboration resembling a political club rather than an economic one. A political club shares work on political-equity criteria, based on bargaining about fair shares, leading to substantial transaction costs (known as *juste retour*). In contrast, with an economic club there would be a prime contractor that would allocate work on the basis of comparative and competitive advantage. For example, if a nation is good at vertical take-off technology, that nation would undertake such work; and if a partner is good at producing aircraft wings, that nation should specialize in producing wings. This model allocates work on the basis of competitiveness and not on some bargaining requirement that each partner should be involved in each aspect of the high technology on the project. Actual international collaboration departs from the ideal economic model and creates inefficiencies in both development and production. Each partner nation will demand its fair share of the advanced technology on the project and a share of production work. The result is duplication in flight-testing centres and duplicate final assembly lines, adding to the costs of international collaboration. Furthermore, the bargaining in political clubs and their decision-making rules leads to project delays. Bureaucracy dominates, with decisions made by large numbers of large international committees, meaning that agreed decisions take time.

Overall, collaboration inefficiencies might lead to development costs being twice those for a similar national alternative, but higher costs are shared between the partner nations (e.g., development costs might double but these are shared over, say, four nations). Inefficiencies in collaborative production work might mean that economies of scale and learning on collaborative programmes might be half of those on a national alternative. Delays also arise, with estimates showing that two-nation collaborations might take more than 25 per cent longer and four-nation collaborations might take almost 60 per cent longer than a similar national project (Hartley 2011a, 2014).

Any economic assessment of international collaboration needs to be based on some alternative procurement option such as a national project. On this basis, international collaboration provides *some* of the military–strategic and wider economic benefits from a national project and these benefits are greater compared with an off-the-shelf foreign buy. Collaboration also leads to greater standardization of arms between the partner nations. However, reservations remain about collaboration.

Critics of collaboration point to the cases of the French Rafale and Swedish Gripen as examples of European nations developing and producing modern combat aircraft on a national basis. But while France and Sweden have demonstrated that they are technologically capable of developing a modern combat aircraft, it is unlikely that they will be willing to fund any future replacement as an independent venture: international collaboration might therefore remain economically attractive. However, there is scope for improving the efficiency of international collaboration by restricting the number of major partners to, say, two nations and by selecting a prime contractor with responsibility for allocating work shares based on competitiveness. In this model, other partner nations could join the collaboration but they would be junior partners and would be awarded supply contracts based on competitiveness (cf. international partnering on the F-35 aircraft). Airbus is an example of a successful international collaboration based on two major partners specializing in large civil aircraft. Nor should it be assumed that all international collaborations should be restricted to European nations. Other countries might be willing to join an international arms partnership (e.g., Australia, Brazil, Canada, India, Japan, South Korea). But willingness to join an international club will depend on the costs of independent national arms projects. Here, arms exports provide an economic means of maintaining a national defence industrial base.

Exports

The international arms trade is controversial. Critics condemn arms sales as contributing to regional arms races and local conflict; arms exports are condemned for supporting oppressive regimes with poor human rights records; and it is claimed that arms exports lead poor nations to allocate resources to arms rather than to promoting economic development. One view is that the arms trade "is a deadly business: it supports conflict and human rights abusing regimes and squanders valuable resources" (CAAT 2016a,b). This is, indeed, an impressive indictment that has to be addressed, analysed and evaluated. What are the facts, what is the real problem, why does it exist, and what can be done about it? A starting point is to consider the facts.

The international arms trade involves nations exporting and importing arms. The resulting transactions are sizeable, as shown by the data in Table 7.2. Immediately it has to be stressed that estimating the world arms trade is fraught with data problems. For example, an arms export can vary from the acquisition of a number of weapons to the purchase of arms and supporting packages (e.g., training, provision of armaments and spares). Price data can also vary, with unit prices based on unit production costs only or including a mark-up for R & D costs. Nonetheless, the data in

Table 7.2 show the major arms exporters and importers. The data are for major weapons only, excluding other groups and the illegal arms trade. Over the period 2010–15, the US and Russia accounted for almost 60 per cent of total arms exports, and the top six arms-exporting countries accounted for some 75 per cent of the total (including China, Germany, France and the UK). There was less concentration among arms importers, with India and Saudi Arabia accounting for 20 per cent of total arms imports and the top ten accounting for almost 50 per cent of the total. In terms of trends over the period 2010–15, arms exports from the US and China increased by some 30 per cent in real terms, while those from Spain increased almost fivefold and those from France more than doubled. Similarly, over the same period, arms imports to Saudi Arabia increased threefold and for the UAE they doubled; conversely, there were substantial reductions in real terms for Pakistan, the US, South Korea and Singapore.

The international arms trade reflects beneficial trade and exchange between buyers and sellers. Such transactions raise questions about who benefits, what are the costs, and is there evidence on the magnitudes of both benefits and costs? The possibility also has to be considered that each party to the transaction might only assess the impact on its national welfare and not on the welfare of other countries. Consider, first, the private benefits. Arms exports by private firms provide benefits in the form of profits for companies and their shareholders. Arms imports enable importing governments to provide peace, protection and national security for their citizens, which economists classify as public goods. However, there might be additional benefits for society and these also need to be considered.

Arms-exporting nations receive additional military, strategic and wider economic benefits. Arms exports contribute to maintaining a national defence industrial base, which provides independence and security of supply. Without exports, a nation would be faced with the costs of maintaining its defence industrial base. Here, the options include the provision of small orders to maintain capacity or the mothballing of some capacity or allowing a complete "rundown" and accepting the costs of rebuilding industrial capacity: all options involve costs and require accurate estimates of the magnitude of such costs. Alternatively, the arms-exporting nation could accept a decline in its national defence industrial base and rely increasingly on importing arms from overseas suppliers with the associated costs.

Table 7.2 World arms trade, 2010–15.

	US$ millions (1990 prices)		
Nation	2010	2015	2010–15
Arms exporter:			
US	8,098	10,484	55,006
Russia	6,172	5,483	42,404
China	1,496	1,966	9,943
Germany	2,745	2,049	9,476
France	898	2,013	8,932
UK	1,151	1,214	7,627
Spain	263	1,279	5,310
Italy	516	570	4,360
Ukraine	470	323	4,156
Israel	686	710	3,280
Total	**25,857**	**28,626**	**168,747**
Arms importer:			
India	3,017	3,078	23,124
Saudi Arabia	1,070	3,161	11,002
China	1,045	1,214	7,726
UAE	605	1,289	7,156
Pakistan	2,176	735	6,899
Australia	1,507	1,574	6,711
Turkey	484	448	5,410
US	1,111	565	5,220
South Korea	1,250	245	5,011
Singapore	1,020	98	4,344
Total	**25,857**	**28,626**	**168,747**

Notes. (i) Value data are based on trade indicator values and are shown in millions of US dollars at constant 1990 prices. Note that trade indicator values show volume data for major weapons only. They do not show value data nor sales prices for arms transfers, and hence they should not be related to GDP and military expenditure data. (ii) Nations ranked on basis of their total arms sales for 2010–15. Totals are based on all nations and not solely on those listed in the table.

Source: SIPRI (2016c).

There are further economic benefits in the form of jobs and export earnings, and possible effects on the unit price of arms for the exporting nation's armed forces. For example, arms exporters might require a payment by the importing nation as a contribution to its R & D costs. Also, increased output due to export sales will reduce the national contribution to a firm's fixed overhead costs and might lead to lower unit production costs of arms for the exporting nation. But such claimed benefits have to be assessed critically. Arms-exporting nations might waive any R & D levy on foreign sales. Also, lower unit production costs for the exporting nation's armed forces only arise where export sales are included in the initial production plans for the exporter or where the exporting nation's armed forces buy additional arms following export sales. However, without arms exports, an exporting nation would have to make a greater contribution to a firm's fixed overhead costs, raising the unit costs of arms purchased for its national armed forces. Arms exports also offer possible political benefits by allowing the exporting nation to influence the behaviour of the importing nation (e.g., by withdrawing arms supplies for "unacceptable" behaviour by the importer).

Arms-exporting nations incur further costs in supporting arms exports. For example, governments of exporting nations provide various forms of financial and non-financial assistance to arms exporters. These might include the provision of loans at favourable interest rates, exemption from the payment of R & D levies, assistance with training, the use of government staff to promote arms exports, and the use of a nation's armed forces in arms promotional activities (e.g., air displays, naval visits to foreign ports). Reductions in arms exports involve further adjustment costs, which might be substantial for some local economies.

Few economic studies have estimated the benefits and costs of arms exports. One study estimated the costs and benefits of a 50 per cent reduction in UK defence exports. The analysis focused on the impacts on UK resident workers, shareholders, the UK government and the associated adjustment costs. It estimated the impacts on job losses in the UK defence export sector and the offsetting job creation in non-defence employment. The study concluded that the economic costs of reducing UK defence exports are relatively small and mostly one-off costs, and that the balance of argument about UK defence exports should depend mainly on non-economic considerations (Chalmers *et al* 2002).

A further 2016 study of UK arms exports found that the UK provided a variety of direct subsidies to arms exports: estimated in the region of £104 million–£142 million annually. It concluded that the UK arms-procurement system behaves as if its primary goal is the preservation and promotion of the UK arms industry (Freeman 2016).

Arms imports also involve benefits and costs for the importing nations. Arms imports provide the importing nation with national benefits through equipment contributing to its protection and national security. Often, in a competitive world market, arms imports are cost-effective: suppliers will enter into fierce competition to obtain substantial arms contracts, leading to relatively low prices. But one cost of arms imports arises where they are associated with corruption in government and business. Where corruption is widespread, it will lead to inefficiencies in the economy and adverse effects on economic growth (e.g., with scarce resources allocated to corrupt activities rather than to efficiency and growth).

Arms imports do not always guarantee a successful product. The Australian army purchased a fleet of Tiger attack helicopters from Airbus Helicopters believing that it was a low-risk off-the-shelf helicopter. A 2016 Australian National Audit Office report was highly critical of the imported Tigers. It found 76 capability deficiencies, of which 60 were regarded as "critical". On average, only 3.5 Tiger helicopters out of an operational fleet of 16 were available on any given day in 2015; this was below the targeted readiness of 12 helicopters. Costs per flying hour were A$30,335 compared with a target of A$20,000. The Tiger's capability as a combat platform was also criticized (e.g., communication problems, weapons availability, cockpit fumes). The result will be the early retirement and replacement of Australia's Tiger helicopters (ANAO 2016).

Critics claim that arms imports add to local and regional tensions, making conflict more likely. But it has to be recognized that nations have a right to acquire arms for their self-defence and that arms races produce complex results, including contributing to peaceful outcomes (cf. peace during the Cold War). Also, arms imports are often the focus of criticisms that reflect confusion between correlation and causation. Some observations about the impact of arms imports and their responsibility for "all the evils of the world" are usually based on simple correlations that ignore the complex variables involved in causation. Critics of the arms trade too often base their case on personal prejudice and value judgements, ignoring the contribution of economic theory and the available empirical evidence.

The world is not perfect and it offers massive opportunities for improvements: even small and modest improvements are welcome. A world without arms would be safer, happier and more prosperous. Reality is different, though, and the world remains unsafe, with myriads of known, unknown and unknowable threats to a nation's population that require internal police forces and armed forces for external protection. Even private households allocate substantial resources to their own security and protection. Examples include home insurance policies, health and car insurance, security cameras and burglar alarms, the purchase of a house in a "safe" area and the purchase of "safe" motor cars that provide protection in the event of a crash. The arms trade has been the focus of policies for its control and regulation.

Controlling the arms trade

Various mechanisms exist to control the international arms trade, including voluntary self-restraint and international agreements. Arms-exporting nations can voluntarily choose to limit their arms exports through price, quantity and quality controls or a total withdrawal and ban on all arms exports or restrictions for specific countries. For example, an arms-exporting nation can impose a high price, limit quantities or place restrictions on specific aspects of quality (e.g., the US allowing exports of Apache helicopters but without their Longbow radars; US restrictions on the export of F-22 combat aircraft and armed UAVs). Alternatively, a nation can refuse to sell arms to certain countries or it can opt out completely from the arms export business, but such export restrictions might encourage foreign nations to develop their own arms industries. Voluntary self-restraint involves costs for the nation imposing the arms export restrictions. The extreme case arises where a nation imposes a complete ban on arms exports so that its national arms producers are confined to sales to its national armed forces. An example is the UK nuclear submarine industry, which supplies small numbers of costly submarines to the UK's Royal Navy. There is a further problem: namely, that other nations might not observe similar arms export restrictions, so that a foreign state continues to receive arms. This resembles a game theory "prisoner's dilemma" situation.

An alternative to voluntary restraint by a single nation involves multilateral and mandatory arms embargoes administered by international agencies such as the UN, the EU and the OSCE. These agreements use sanctions to change the behaviour of states, to limit their available resources for conflict, or to signal disapproval of a nation's behaviour. Examples have included arms embargoes imposed on nations such as Armenia, Belarus, Iran, Syria, Myanmar, North Korea, Russia and Zimbabwe. South Africa was also subject to such an embargo over the period 1977–94. International arms embargoes are subject to at least two problems. First, there is the definition of arms and dual-use goods. Some goods can be cheaply and quickly converted from civilian to military use. Examples include small trucks, which can be equipped with rocket launchers so that they can readily be used as light armoured fighting vehicles; jet airliners and civilian helicopters can be used as troop transporters; and oil tankers can be converted into aircraft carriers for helicopters and vertical take-off combat aircraft. Second, illegal trading allows embargoed nations to obtain arms. Illegal trading arises where arms might be supplied by private traders or by governments that refuse to accept an international arms embargo. Examples of such nations include China, North Korea, Pakistan and Russia.

There are a number of international treaties and agreements on arms exports, including the Arms Trade Treaty, the Wassenaar Arrangement and the EU Common Position on Arms Exports. The Arms Trade Treaty of 2014 is a multilateral treaty that regulates the international trade in conventional weapons, ranging from small arms to main battle tanks and combat aircraft. It aims to monitor arms exports and ensure compliance with arms embargoes. Five of the world's top arms exporters have signed the treaty, including France, Germany, Italy, Spain and the UK. The Wassenaar Arrangement (July 1996) relates to arms export controls for conventional arms and dual-use goods and technologies. It aims at regional and international security and stability by promoting transparency and greater responsibility in transfers of arms and dual-use goods and technologies, including preventing their acquisition by terrorists. It has been signed by such nations as France, Germany, Italy, Russia, the UK and the US, but it is not a treaty and is therefore not legally binding. The EU Common

Position on Arms Exports of 1998 is a legally binding regional agreement on conventional arms exports. It requires all EU member states to have a licence system for arms exports and to contribute to the EU Annual Report on Arms Exports. The aim is to establish a code of conduct to harmonize member states' arms export policies under the framework of the Common Foreign and Security Policy of the EU.

International treaties and agreements make a useful contribution to controlling arms exports but they have their limitations. First, reaching an international agreement is not costless and involves significant transaction and policing costs as well as other economic costs (e.g., loss of arms exports). Second, not all nations are signatories to such agreements. Third, they might not be legally enforceable, and there is no international agency with the legal powers to enforce such agreements. Fourth, agreements are subject to substitution effects as nations seek alternative types of weapons that are not subject to arms export controls.

Improving procurement efficiency

Whichever procurement option is chosen, the purchasing government has the challenge of achieving efficiency in its procurement. Decisions are required on whether there will be competition for the contract and the form of contract for the purchase. Often, competition and fixed-price contracts are the preferred options for efficient procurement. Of course, government might adopt a wider definition of efficiency, departing from any economic criteria (claiming that, by definition, all their decisions are efficient!).

The life cycle of a new weapons project involves design, development, production, in-service operations and disposal. In principle, competition is possible at each stage of the life cycle, where competition might be restricted to domestic firms or extended to allow bids by foreign arms producers. At the design stage, competition is usually based on design criteria where a number of firms might be invited to bid. Next, the project proceeds to the development phase, where two or more firms might be invited to build technology demonstrators or competing prototypes (e.g., fly-before-you-buy). At the end of development, the successful firm might be promised a production contract for all the required units or for a limited number only, with the residual production order subject to competition. Finally, mid-life updates and disposal can also be subject to competition. However, proposals for introducing competition at later stages in the project life cycle are not without their problems. Competition for production work should favour the original developer, who has access to all the relevant production technology, over a new entrant, who lacks detailed information on the project design. In the circumstances, an original developer will not be legally required to provide more than the basic drawings and design to rivals, and the developer will be unwilling to transfer any technology that was privately funded. In these circumstances, the technology transfer required by competition can be problematic and costly. Often, much technology is embodied in a firm's human capital and is not easily transferable in the form of drawings and designs.

At each stage where competition is used to award a contract, further choices are required on the form of contract. The options range from fixed-price to cost-plus to target-cost incentive contracts, each with different efficiency incentives. Fixed-price contracts form high-powered incentive schemes compared with cost-plus contracts, which are low-powered incentive schemes, while target-cost contracts provide intermediate incentives between the extremes. Fixed-price contracts differ from firm-price contracts, with the former allowing price variations to reflect inflation in labour and materials input costs. In contrast, firm-price contracts allow no price variations. Nations use different terminology when classifying contracts (e.g., firm-fixed-price contracts).

Efforts to improve procurement efficiency have led to attempts to introduce fixed-price contracts into each stage of a weapons project's life cycle. An extreme example occurred in the US in the mid-1960s with the introduction of "total package procurement", where a single fixed-price contract was awarded for design, development, production and support, embracing price, performance and delivery commitments. US examples included contracts for the Air Force C-5 military aircraft transporter and for the US Navy's Tarawa amphibious assault ships and its Spruance-class destroyers. These contracts were a reaction to the previous cost-plus regime: they aimed to end the practice of firms deliberately bidding low prices to win a competition and they aimed to end "optimism bias". In practice, they encountered major design and technical problems, leading to cost overruns and delays.

The C-5 Galaxy military transport aircraft was a classic example of the problems with total package procurement. In 1964, the US Air Force received proposals from five airframe firms which it down-selected to three firms, with each awarded a one-year study contract. Eventually, Lockheed was awarded a contract, mainly because it submitted the lowest total cost bid, leading to a total package procurement contract. However, Lockheed experienced cost overruns and technical difficulties that led to major financial problems, and government loans were required to keep the company operational. Eventually, in 1970, the US abandoned total package procurement except in rare situations. In contrast, the UK used total package procurement successfully for the acquisition of its Hawk jet trainer aircraft.

Where governments decide to buy arms without competition, they still have to determine the type of contract to be awarded. Non-competitive contracts require the procurement agency to determine prices and profits for such contracts: typically, competition "solves" these problems. Non-competitive cost-plus contracts represent extremely low-powered schemes. Firms recover all their actual costs with profits based on a percentage of those actual costs: such contracts are often used for risky and uncertain development work. In contrast, non-competitive fixed-price contracts provide greater efficiency incentives: they are based on estimated costs and a profit allowance and are often used for less risky production work (where the unknowns are reduced).

Non-competitive contracts require government regulatory rules on profitability. For example, the UK's Single Source Regulations Office determines profitability on non-competitive contracts. In 2014/15, such contracts accounted for 53 per cent of the value of new Ministry of Defence contracts. Officially, single-source contracts are awarded where there is only a single contractor, where there are strong reasons for retaining a national capability, where there are issues of national security, and where the product or service has special or unique features. In 2016, the UK applied a baseline profit rate of 8.95 per cent on cost for its non-competitive contracts. This profit rate was based on the comparability principle: namely, comparisons with the profitability of a similar group of companies comprising an international and appropriate group (SSRO 2016a).

Further policies are available to improve the efficiency of arms procurement. Procurement agencies can import modern business practices from private commercial firms. Examples include partnering agreements with prime contractors, the adoption of modern management accounting methods, and the use of external management consultants to assess the cost estimates of arms producers. Procurement staff might be seconded to private firms to gain business skills, and these staff might be rewarded through greater use of salary related to contract outcomes against targets. Experiments with the use of greater incentive systems in procurement contracts can be undertaken: for example, varying profit rates related to contractor productivity and innovation. Care is needed to avoid unexpected and undesirable outcomes. It also has to be recognized that importing private sector business practices into a defence department might not, by itself, be successful without recognizing the incentive systems in the private sector: namely, the profit motive, competition and the role of the capital market as a policing and monitoring mechanism.

How to thwart rules for efficient buying

Governments are always seeking procurement policies that improve the efficiency of their arms buying. Arms producers will respond by using measures to thwart the aims of such policies. Consider the examples of competition and fixed-price contracts often advocated to improve the efficiency of arms purchases.

Competition for arms contracts is often presented as a means of improving the efficiency of arms producers, with predictions of lower prices, better quality and market-determined profitability. But there might be market constraints on achieving competition. Also, arms producers are not passive agents and their responses can thwart the government's aims. There are at least four constraints on competition policy.

First, the losing firm in a competition can always acquire the winning firm (depending on a nation's merger policy). Second, once a competition has led to the award of a contract, the winning firm becomes a monopoly supplier. Third, arms producers can bid a low competitive price and then "cross-subsidize" a loss-making contract by recovering losses on the winning contract through other arms contracts (e.g., servicing, spares, exports). Fourth, the domestic arms industry might be dominated by national monopoly suppliers. Introducing competition into such a market requires that foreign firms be allowed to bid for national defence contracts. Competitive bidding is not costless and if foreign firms are to continue bidding, they will need some reasonable prospect that they will be successful (i.e. that they are not to be used as "stalking horses"). However, national arms producers will lobby government to award the contract to its national champion. Or, if the contract is awarded to a foreign firm, there will be adverse economic impacts on the domestic defence industrial base. Domestic arms producers will be the losers from a foreign buy and they will seek compensation through some form of offset work that might be "trade-distorting".

Fixed-price contracts also have their limitations. They appear to offer high-powered incentives, where the firm is the residual claimant for its cost savings and bears all the costs of any overruns. Much depends on whether arms producers believe that the contract will always be imposed. For example, such contracts are often revised to reflect modifications and new requirements, some of which might arise from arms producer behaviour (e.g., offering military procurement staff an attractive modification that leads to a contract change and a price revision). Or, where cost overruns on fixed-price contracts result in a major arms producer facing the prospect of bankruptcy and industry exit, the government might intervene and bail it out (some large arms firms might be too big to fail). A bailout effectively converts a fixed-price contract into a cost-plus contract, thereby losing all efficiency incentives.

The law can also interfere with the competitive process. Consider the example of the competition for the USAF air tanker. Traditionally, Boeing always supplied air tankers for the USAF. In 2008, Boeing and a joint team of Northrop Grumman and Airbus submitted bids for the air tanker contract. The Northrop Grumman–Airbus team was selected. However, Boeing protested to the General Accountability Office (GAO) and started a public relations campaign in support of their protest. In June 2008, the USAF admitted flaws in the bidding process and the GAO upheld Boeing's protest and recommended that the contract be re-bid. In 2009, the USAF started a new round of bidding with clearer and simpler criteria. At this stage, Airbus bid without Northrop Grumman as a partner. In early 2011, the USAF selected Boeing as the successful bidder, reversing its original contract decision.

A similar appeal arose over the contract award for the US B-21 bomber. Following a competition between Northrop Grumman and a Boeing– Lockheed Martin team, the contract was awarded to Northrop Grumman. The Boeing team challenged the contract award, claiming that the selection process was "fundamentally flawed". The case was reviewed by the GAO, which found no basis to sustain or uphold the protest. The GAO found that the technical evaluation and the evaluation of costs were reasonable, consistent with the terms of the competition and in accordance with procurement laws and regulations. As a result, Northrop Grumman was confirmed as the contract winner but the appeal delayed the project by three months.

Arms producers are not the only barrier to improving the efficiency of arms procurement. Government staff are not passive, unresponsive agents. They are also a barrier to change: they will aim to protect their position through their willingness to play any games. They will use emotive language to protect their jobs and status. For example, they will claim that their activity is "vital" to the national interest, that change will have adverse effects on national security, and that the output of defence cannot be measured and cannot be subject to "vulgar" cost–benefit analysis (see Chapter 8).

Military–strategic and wider economic benefits

Governments can interfere with arms procurement choices. Often, they interfere where there are believed to be military–strategic benefits from a national procurement. Examples include the French, UK and US desire to retain a nuclear submarine industry that includes suppliers of "key" components or materials as well as the supplier of the nuclear power plant (e.g., Rolls-Royce in the UK). Or, government might wish to retain a warship building yard, or a sole supplier of tanks, or an aircraft design and production plant. Such industrial capabilities provide independence and security of supply, especially in conflict. But retaining industrial capacity is not a free gift. Costs are involved and choices are required between retaining various industrial capabilities. The price of retaining a nuclear submarine industry might be the loss of a national tank producer or a national warship yard (something has to go).

Buying arms from national producers also appears to offer wider economic benefits in the form of jobs, technology, spin-offs and contributions to the balance of payments through import-savings. An example occurred in early 1965 when the UK Labour government decided to buy the maritime version of the Comet, known as the Nimrod MR1. At the time, the choice was between a British aircraft and two off-the-shelf foreign options: namely, the Lockheed Orion and the French Breguet Atlantic. However, France was only willing to transfer a maximum of 21 per cent of the Atlantic build programme to the UK, which was regarded as an insufficient financial incentive to buy the aircraft. Eventually, the British Nimrod was selected against a background of the cancellation of major UK aircraft projects. The Nimrod was offered at a similar price to the Atlantic and was presented as offering much better value for money, which satisfied the Treasury. It achieved political targets and provided an economically beneficial project through its impact on the balance of trade and domestic aviation industry employment (Yonge 2013).

The wider economic benefits from buying from national arms producers appear attractive, but appearances can be deceptive. Economists criticize such wider economic benefits by identifying alternative and more cost-effective policies to achieve the same objectives. For example, large-scale construction projects create jobs (e.g., building hospitals, houses, schools and roads). Also, economists assess the case for state intervention by focusing on market failure and the appropriate public policies to correct such failures and improve the operation of markets. Furthermore, a focus on wider economic benefits is not the concern of defence policy objectives, which, instead, provide peace, protection and security.

Conclusion

Ideally, any economic assessment of arms buying needs to consider the relationship between defence inputs, including arms, and the resulting defence output. Here, there are large unknowns, requiring much more analytical and empirical work. A study of the performance of European armed forces based on various indicators found that the UK scored high on all measures (Beeres & Bogers 2012).

Overall, arms producers will adapt and adjust to any new policies aimed at improving their efficiency. For instance, the application of performance indicators appears an attractive solution, but there are likely to be unexpected and undesirable outcomes. In the case of the health service, the use of performance indicators might lead to a focus on successful operations despite the patient having died! Greater understanding of the arms industry can be obtained by focusing on the military–industrial–political complex.

Notes

1. Duplicate projects can comprise large-scale development of two projects or a much cheaper system of limited technology demonstrators for a number of projects.
2. For example, with two competing developers, each development project might cost, say, $1 billion: hence, the argument that a single developer might result in savings of $1 billion. But a single developer is a monopoly lacking a competitive stimulus to minimize costs, so its development costs might be, say, $1.5 billion rather than the expected $1 billion for a given project.

8

THE MILITARY–INDUSTRIAL–POLITICAL COMPLEX

Introduction

Arms industries are often condemned for being part of a powerful military–industrial complex that determines arms decisions. Is this a figment of the imagination or a real feature of arms industries? Developments in the economics of politics and public choice analysis provide valuable insights into understanding this complex.

The term is associated with President Eisenhower's farewell address in January 1961, when he referred to the need for society to "guard against the acquisition of unwarranted influence ... by the military–industrial complex", adding that "the potential for the disastrous rise of misplaced power exists and will persist" (Eisenhower 1961). The political component has been added to the description military–industrial complex to recognize the role of political markets within the complex. Political markets comprise governments, political parties, bureaucracies and various other interest groups consisting of producers, consumers, and the disarmament, peace, environmental and green movements. This approach departs from the traditional economic model of competitive markets assuming large numbers of buyers and sellers. Instead, arms industries operate in political markets where the government is the only or major buyer and where there are often monopoly or oligopoly suppliers with barriers to new entry and markets typically in disequilibrium rather than achieving some neat mathematical and theoretical equilibrium.

A further political dimension arises where arms producers are state owned rather than privately owned. The result of arms industries operating in political markets is that we need to use public choice analysis to further understand and explain behaviour in such markets.

A public choice approach

Public choice analysis explains behaviour in political markets using the concepts of self-interest and mutually beneficial exchange operating within the rules determined by the constitution or by some other rule-making individual or group. It involves the application of economics to political science and studies non-market decision-making. The analysis identifies various agents within democratic political markets, consisting of voters, political parties, governments, bureaucracies and interest groups. Each agent will pursue its own self-interest, which will determine its preferences for public policies towards arms industries. Examples include the choice of which arms to buy, from which contractor (national or foreign), how the arms will be bought (choice of contract) and at what price and profitability.

Political markets resemble other markets, with buyers and sellers undertaking transactions leading to individual and group decision-making; but there is one major difference. Political markets do not replicate competitive markets, where the outcomes of decisions result in a set of prices and outputs; public choice analysis does, though, produce hypotheses about the outcomes of political transactions. Initially, a major transaction concerns the choice of the society's voting rules (i.e. its constitution), with options ranging from unanimity to various forms of majority voting rules, where the aim is to select a winning candidate at elections. Different voting rules have different efficiency outcomes (Mueller 1989).

Voters

In public choice models, voters are like consumers and are assumed to seek the maximum benefits from the policies offered by rival political parties. Voters will vote for politicians who maximize their gains from government and minimize their tax burdens (and maximize their state welfare payments). However, many voters are not well informed about defence, arms and other issues involved in the election. Such voters are likely to be influenced by specialist producer and other interest groups who are able to afford to invest in acquiring costly information and knowledge about defence and arms policies. Examples include arms producers using their specialist knowledge to show that buying national arms represents "good value for money", providing independence, national security and protection as well as jobs, technology and balance of payments contributions. Similarly, arms producers will present major weapons programmes as "vital" for national security, with such examples as the US F-35 combat aircraft programme and the UK decision to replace its Trident nuclear system. Such claims will be reinforced by other interest groups, including NATO member states. In contrast, anti-arms and anti-war groups (e.g., CND, CAAT) will oppose arms spending and will campaign for the cancellation of major arms projects.

Public choice models also predict that the voters who are best informed on a specific issue are those whose income is directly affected by it: hence, employees of arms companies are more likely to be informed of arms issues. Some of these propositions about voter behaviour have been criticized for being based on unrealistic assumptions, including voter rationality, and for confusing descriptive reality for explanatory power. Problems also arise since voting is not costless and its likely benefits to an individual voter are probably negligible (why do people vote?). Nonetheless, the analysis shows the limitations of various voting systems as a means of identifying society's views and valuations on specific policies such as arms spending and support for arms producers. Typically, elections require voters to choose alternative bundles of policies where arms spending is only one component of the package and where voters cannot register their willingness to pay for each policy element. In the UK in 1997, the Labour Party in opposition promised a Defence Review as its defence policy, with the review only completed *after* it was elected.

Referenda appear an attractive alternative for making social choices but they usually involve only binary choices, with no indications of the valuations placed on each option and its ranking among all other choices. For example, a referendum held on nuclear weapons policy might produce an outcome abandoning such weapons, but this choice would not allow society any consideration of the relative weighting (valuation) of nuclear weapons compared with a range of alternative conventional arms programmes or other public or private spending (via lower taxes).[1] Referenda also need to be viewed as a government choice appearing to offer society a role in "important" decision-making, but in reality they reflect the government's continued desire to win elections. A real-world arms procurement example occurred with the Swiss referendum on its decision to purchase the Swedish Gripen fighter aircraft. The 2014 referendum rejected the Swiss government's plans to buy the Gripen without providing any guidance on the country's need for a new combat aircraft.

Governments and political parties

Public choice models assume that in democracies, political parties are vote maximizers. They behave like firms offering policies and legislation in exchange for votes. Politicians are assumed to be motivated by self-interest, reflected in the income, power and prestige that results from being in office: they formulate policies to win elections. The party that forms the government arranges its policies to gain it the most votes within the constraints of the constitution. Governments then seek re-election. In this model, vote-maximizing politicians will favour debt-financed public expenditure, where taxpayers cannot identify their contribution to the costs of inflationary finance, with arms spending comprising one component of public expenditure.

The model offers some testable predictions. First, in a two-party democratic system, both political parties will aim to satisfy the preferences of the median voter and both parties will agree on issues favoured by a majority of voters. Second, it is predicted that the policies of democratic governments tend to favour producers more than consumers (Downs 1957). All this assumes legal behaviour and can be changed where corruption and illegal and criminal actions affect government decisions. An extreme example is the role of the Mafia and criminal gangs in determining local, regional and national decisions (via bribery, threats, intimidation and assassinations).

The winning party or president at an election captures the entire market and forms the government (cf. a monopoly for the elected term). Its policies are then implemented by government bureaucracies.

Bureaucracies: the armed forces and defence departments

Government bureaucracies supply the elected government with alternative administrative packages to achieve its policy aims. Defence has two sets of bureaucracies: namely, the armed forces and the national defence department or defence ministry, each of which forms an interest group. Other government departments might also have an interest in defence decisions, including the departments of industry, business, innovation, education, employment and overseas trade.

Economic models of bureaucracy start by assuming that bureaucracies are budget maximizers. Larger budgets enable bureaucrats to satisfy their personal preferences for salaries, job security, power, patronage and prestige, and on-the-job leisure disguised as output. Government departments such as defence have incentives to use their budgets or lose them. Where budgets are allocated for a fiscal year, a defence department has every incentive to spend all its allocated funds, even if this means inefficient end-of-year spending of any residual budget. Such behaviour is summarized in the conventional wisdom of "use it or lose it" (Hurley *et al* 2014). There are no incentives to save on budget spending: savings mean smaller departments and a reduction in a department's power, influence and status.

The desire for a larger budget is limited by the requirement that the bureau's budget covers its costs of production. Within the military–political complex there are two sets of bureaucracies: namely, the armed forces and the defence department or defence ministry. In this context, the armed forces can be viewed as *agents*, with the defence department being the *principal*. In turn, the defence department is in an agent relationship with the government, which can be regarded as its principal; but ultimately, voters are the principal with government as their agent. The principal–agent problem identifies the difficulties of the principal or owner monitoring the activities of an agent to whom decisions have been delegated (prospects arise of agents fooling their masters (Peacock 1992: 82)).

Numerous examples have arisen of principal–agent problems in the military sector. Governments as principals issue orders to the military to pursue specific objectives; but problems arise where such objectives are far from clear and the military sector adapts the orders to pursue its preferred objectives. During the Second World War, there were numerous examples of senior Allied commanders pursuing their own objectives, as occurred over the strategic bombing of Germany (e.g., a preference for bombing German cities rather than industrial targets). The behaviour of senior Allied commanders was also influenced by their personalities and egos, with cravings for fame, public recognition and adoration. Examples included Generals MacArthur, Montgomery and Patton, and Air Marshals Tedder and Coningham; Montgomery was reported to have had poor relations with every other senior Allied commander in the war (Rait 2016). Similarly, inter-service rivalry affects behaviour and the use of military force. For example, during the Vietnam War, US forces fought the war for which they were postured, trained and equipped and relied on metrics to measure effectiveness, with metrics becoming the end in itself (e.g., the numbers of bombs dropped, the amount of napalm delivered, the number of villages destroyed). But performance metrics can lead to unexpected and undesirable results. For example, after delivering x numbers of bombs, it was assumed that the enemy Viet Cong had been killed and defeated: reality was different, with enemy soldiers continually appearing and continuing to fight!

Also, in the Vietnam War, strike aircraft provided by the US Air Force and Navy were organizationally independent throughout the war and counterinsurgency operations were conducted with the existing equipment, which was not the most effective way of fighting such a conflict. Inter-service rivalry between the Air Force and the Navy in the use of air power led to competition over sortie counts and targets destroyed. Further inter-service rivalry occurred between the Air Force and the US Army over the effectiveness of Army-operated helicopter gunships and Air Force-operated aircraft gunships. In addition, the US policy of using firepower rather than ground troops had some counterproductive effects and unintended consequences. Aerial firepower destroyed villages and killed and injured civilians and their cattle, on which they relied for their livelihood. The result was to create a constituency for the Viet Cong, which also supplied the displaced villagers with food and shelter.

A similar result occurred in Germany in the Second World War when, following the Allied bombing of cities, the Nazi regime provided food and shelter for basic survival (Shaw 2016). The Afghanistan war of 2001–14 provided yet another example when allied troops destroyed the local opium crops, which led to local farmers supporting the Taliban. Overall, the poppy eradication programme was ineffective and counterproductive, giving the Taliban a decisive advantage in obtaining support from the local people. Opium production in Afghanistan was a major source of funding for the Taliban. US efforts at eradication were thwarted by corruption and power relations in Afghanistan (e.g., rich farmers bribed themselves out of trouble, leaving poor farmers to bear all the adjustment costs, which was considered unfair). Conflict destroyed the legitimate economic sector, leading to the development of the illegal economy based on criminal enterprise and corruption. The drug industry provided better salaries than the legal economy and profits from the drug trade funded the Taliban's role in the conflict.

Economic models of bureaucracy provide predictions that explain the behaviour of the armed forces and defence departments. Bureaucracies are monopoly suppliers of information and services to governments. Government can be viewed as buying protection from its national defence department, which will be the sole supplier of information and defence services. External protection is supplied by the armed forces, specializing in air, land and sea forces, with each seeking to protect its traditional monopoly property rights in these domains. The model predicts that budget maximization will lead the defence department to exaggerate the threat, underestimate costs and formulate programmes that are attractive to vote-conscious governments. Bureaucracies as monopolies are also likely to be inefficient in supplying their services. Examples have arisen where the enemy's missile threat and threats from weapons of mass destruction have been exaggerated (e.g., the UK's justification for its role in the Iraq War). In bidding for funds from a limited defence budget, each of the armed forces will offer optimistic cost estimates (optimism bias) on the basis that, once started, projects are difficult to stop. Or, in seeking to protect their budgets, the armed forces might offer optimistic advice on their probability of success in a conflict. Examples of such optimism include the British Army and its interventions in Afghanistan and Iraq in 2003 and 2005. Similarly, senior generals in both World Wars were optimistic about their chances of success, as in the continued battle of the Somme (1916) and the repeated attacks on Caen in 1944 with the loss of French civilian life in the area.

The Chilcot Report on the Iraq War concluded that the UK joined the invasion of Iraq before all peaceful options had been exhausted, that the threat posed by Iraq's President Saddam Hussein had been deliberately exaggerated when no imminent threat existed, and that the UK had made an unconditional and unnecessary commitment to support the US "whatever". Moreover, the report stressed that the UK intelligence community had not tested its sources rigorously enough and that the UK military had not prepared adequately for the aftermath of combat operations. The operation was inadequately resourced and the UK never deployed sufficient forces to create security. The UK Ministry of Defence was further criticized for failing to provide the right equipment and for allowing a second front to be opened in Afghanistan before the situation in Iraq had been stabilized (so breaching its own planning assumptions (Chilcot 2016; Elliott 2016)).

Bureaucracies might also influence industry structure and the size of firms. The dominance of government as a buyer (e.g., in defence markets) encourages the growth of countervailing power through the merger of suppliers. It may also be in the interests of bureaucrats to support such extensions of market imperfections since it may be simpler and more convenient to negotiate with a few dominant suppliers. Organizing and monitoring a genuine competition imposes substantial transaction costs on bureaucracies! Similarly, bureaucracies confronted with information problems when awarding contracts and subsidies to arms producers on the basis of beneficial externalities know that the only effective source of information on the potential performance of the firm is the firm itself (Peacock 1992: 82).

Mechanisms exist for controlling bureaucracies. Examples include pressure groups and investigations by constitutional bodies (e.g., congressional and Senate committees, the UK Parliamentary Defence Committee) and the UK public inquiry into the Iraq war (Chilcot 2016). Or a bureau can be disbanded or acquired by another bureau. The inefficiency of bureaucracies can be exposed to external checks by subjecting their activities to competitive tendering from private contractors. Military outsourcing is an example where functions traditionally undertaken by the armed forces are exposed to rivalry from private firms. A further possibility is to promote competition between bureaux to replace their tendency to promote collusion. The armed forces are a good example, where their small numbers promote collusion rather than competition when faced with cuts in defence budgets. Also, in some societies, possibilities arise of corruption in bureaucracies, leading to such behaviour as replacing equipment that remains in working order or acquiring further equipment that will never be used (Peacock 1992: 158–9).

Critics of the economic model of bureaucracy suggest that the single-minded pursuit of budgets seems inappropriate. Instead, bureaucrats will be concerned with other benefits such as reputation, protecting their department's position, a pleasant working environment, employment of large numbers of staff, and on-the-job leisure, reflected in attendance at international conferences and entertainment of foreign counterparts. Collaborative arms programmes provide opportunities for such international travel and hospitality. Examples of collaborative programmes offering opportunities for international travel include the three-nation Tornado project, the four-nation Typhoon project and the seven-nation A400M airlifter project. Bureaucrats might also seek lucrative private sector employment as well as retirement honours (e.g., a peerage or knighthood in retirement). This view regards bureaucrats as "satisficers" rather than maximizers (Peacock 1992: 76).

Producer groups

Public choice analysis of the military–industrial complex recognizes the influence of producer interest groups in formulating and influencing arms policies. Producer groups will seek monopoly profits, which are also known as rents. Government can help to create, increase or protect a firm's monopoly position, and the resulting monopoly profits or rents form a prize worth pursuing. Arms firms as producer interest groups will seek to acquire monopoly positions by influencing policy in their favour through lobbying, advertising, consultancy reports and support for politicians. Firms will invest in increasing their bargaining skills with government by hiring experienced former public officials who know how government works. Producer groups will also seek to "capture" regulatory agencies, leading to such agencies benefiting producers rather than consumers. There is a further possibility: namely, that in some cases, arms decisions might be influenced by illegal payments in the form of bribes and payments in kind (e.g., holidays, free gifts such as motor cars and rent-free apartments), but such corruption is not confined to arms industries.

Rent seeking by arms producers will aim to influence the award of government arms contracts and military outsourcing contracts. Firms seeking arms contracts will use lobbying and political party donations to influence the award of such contracts, with the prediction that those making such donations will be awarded contracts. On this view, the national defence budget can be regarded as a massive rent available to those who exert the greatest political influence. Rents are also available through tariff protection, subsidies and preferential government purchasing (i.e. buying from national champions). Arms producers will claim that buying from a national firm will lead to a variety of military and economic benefits in such forms as jobs, technology, spin-offs and exports, while also contributing to a firm's monopoly profits (Mueller 1989: Chapter 13)! For example, Lockheed Martin claims that its F-35 Lightning II combat aircraft will support 146,000 direct and indirect US jobs. It also provides employment estimates for each US state (Lockheed Martin 2016): the F-35 programme will support some 38,900 jobs in Texas, where Lockheed Martin is based; some 22,000 jobs in California; and a mere ten jobs in Wisconsin (as well as a further 24,000 jobs in the UK). Such employment estimates appear impressive but it is not unknown for the numbers to be exaggerated, especially for the numbers of indirect jobs. Nor should employment estimates divert attention from other features of the F-35 programme: namely, its cost overruns, delivery delays and performance problems.

Arms producers are sometimes classed as "powerful and influential producer groups", but the concept has not been operationalized. They are likely to be powerful where they are large firms measured by sales and employment and where they are domestic monopoly suppliers. Further indicators of power are the firm's dependence on defence business, its location in marginal constituencies and in high-unemployment areas, and its dependence on non-competitive defence contracts (leading to frequent contacts with national procurement agents). Firms will lobby for large arms contracts by threatening plant closures before an election. For example, the UK decision to replace its Trident nuclear deterrent submarines has been partly justified by claims that cancellation will lead to large numbers of job losses and threaten the future of Barrow-in-Furness, where the submarines will be built. Arms producers also lobby government as a group, reflected in their membership of specialist trade associations, such as those representing aerospace, electronics, naval equipment and land equipment.

Other interest groups

There are other interest groups in the military–industrial–political complex that seek to influence arms spending. Some groups, such as NATO, favour increased arms spending while others oppose such spending. Opposition to arms spending comes from peace, environmental and green movements and from groups opposed to war and nuclear weapons. Forming an interest group is not costless. Costs arise in identifying like-minded people willing to pay the transaction costs involved in creating and maintaining an interest group, especially where some individuals will be "free riders".

Security and defence policy in the European Union provides an example of a complex lobbying network, embracing all institutions responsible for the Common Security and Defence Policy. These include the European Council, the European Commission, the European Parliament and the European Defence Agency as well as organizations representing industries and think tanks in the member states. Specific examples include the AeroSpace and Defence Industries Association of Europe, which represents Europe's aeronautical, spatial, security and defence industries; Airbus Group; and the Security and Defense Agenda, which is a Brussels-based think tank that organizes conferences and debates and publishes reports with policy recommendations (Ruiz *et al* 2016).

Examples

Public choice analysis provides an analytical framework for understanding the military–industrial–political complex. It offers various predictions about political parties favouring the median voter and favouring producers more than consumers, and about governments awarding contracts to arms producers located in marginal constituencies and high-unemployment areas. Bureaucracies aiming to maximize their budgets are likely to be too large and inefficient. Five examples based on the armed forces as bureaucracies, military outsourcing, the behaviour of arms firms in contracting, industrial strategy, and the costs of wars illustrate the application of public choice analysis.

Armed forces

The armed forces as bureaucracies are monopoly suppliers of specialist information and services and they will use this information to their advantage. They will hoard valuable information from their principals (a defence ministry or government) and they will formulate a set of myths around their preferred policies. For example, the armed forces will underestimate the costs of their preferred arms projects and exaggerate their military–strategic and economic benefits. They will support "optimistic" cost estimates and neglect life cycle costs, claiming that they are impossible to estimate. They will also assert that their favoured arms project is "vital" for national security and protection. Once started, major arms projects are difficult to stop: they attract support from interest groups of scientists, contractors, unions and military personnel, each with relative income gains from the continuation of the project. In the case of international collaborative arms projects, it is sometimes claimed that one of their benefits is that they are much more difficult to cancel!

One further aspect of armed forces bureaucratic behaviour can be identified. They have personal preferences for specific types of arms. On this basis, air forces favour advanced-technology manned combat aircraft over unmanned systems and missiles, and they will favour manned combat aircraft over helicopters and transport aircraft. Navies prefer aircraft carriers and warships over support vessels, while armies will favour main battle tanks over supply vehicles. The pursuit of personal military preferences in arms procurement makes it difficult for a government to obtain independent advice on the contribution of various arms projects to national defence and protection. The armed forces as a group form a small numbers game, where there are incentives to collude rather than compete for defence budgets. Such behaviour by the armed forces reflects their desire to retain their traditional monopoly property rights in their specialist domain. Air forces will use all available information to prevent armies from undertaking some of their roles (e.g., ground-based missiles operated by the army replacing air force manned fighter aircraft for air defence missions). Similarly, navies will use all their power and influence to prevent the air force from performing tasks traditionally undertaken by navies. For example, anti-submarine tasks undertaken by frigates rather than by air force maritime patrol aircraft, and naval opposition to land-based aircraft replacing carrier-based aircraft. Armies will also seek to expand their activities into areas traditionally preserved for air forces. For example, army attack helicopters replacing air force manned combat aircraft in close air support tasks, while air forces will claim that their close air support aircraft can replace the army's tanks.

Outsourcing

Military outsourcing can also be analysed using public choice models. Traditionally, the armed forces have undertaken a variety of activities "in-house", such as training, repair and maintenance of their equipment and a range of other support functions. These activities form public sector monopolies protected from competition. Outsourcing, or competitive tendering or privatization, allows private firms to bid for contracts to undertake such activities. The result of competition is improved efficiency, lower prices, innovation, quality improvements and lower profits or reduced organizational slack (e.g., less on-the-job leisure). For example, the outsourcing of military pilot training has led to an emphasis on the cost-effectiveness of such training, reflected in a greater use of flight simulators replacing costly flying training, reduced numbers of training aircraft, fewer bases, smaller numbers of supporting ground crew, and a system of payment for numbers of pilots reaching the required training standard (i.e. rewarding outputs rather than inputs).

Similar new solutions have emerged for the outsourcing of repair and maintenance activities, with private contractors rewarded for the numbers of equipment that are readily available for use by the armed forces (e.g., numbers of aircraft, tanks or warships available per day). The use of military outsourcing has led to innovation, with private contractors offering new ideas and solutions to tasks that the military have not reviewed and assessed for many years. For example, private firms might offer to manage all the services within a military base, rather than a single service such as catering.

A further example concerns the UK's experience with the outsourcing to a private contractor of its military air tanker operations. One unique feature of this example concerns the contractor's willingness to provide a basic fleet of air tankers plus a further number of tankers that are leased to other operators but can be reallocated to the RAF in the event of a conflict (so minimizing the costs of maintaining spare capacity for emergencies). On this basis, outsourcing led to a 27-year contract with a private firm to supply services without requiring the ownership of costly assets (cf. car hire business). It also leads to civilian personnel replacing military personnel, thereby allowing the armed forces to focus on their core functions of war fighting (Hartley 2011a).

Military outsourcing has its critics. The armed forces see private contractors replacing their traditional functions and receiving some of their budgets. They will create a variety of objections to outsourcing, claiming that it means a loss of quality and reliability and that successful private contractors will form a monopoly, leading to a private monopoly replacing a public monopoly. They will object to defence provided for profits and they will demand that their "in-house" units be allowed to bid in any competitions, that all bidders be subject to the same rules of the game, and that competitions should be "properly managed" (managed competition). It will also be pointed out that governments are able to borrow the finance for the project more cheaply than a private contractor; however, political pressures may lead government to move their borrowing "off the balance sheet". The ultimate criticism of outsourcing is that private firms are unreliable and can be declared bankrupt, leaving the armed forces to reconstitute the activity. Each of these criticisms has to be addressed. For example, the armed forces "in-house" activity will never be made bankrupt since its costs, at whatever level, will always be covered by taxpayers (soft budget constraints). Nor can budget constraints be ignored: the armed forces can have any amount of activities supplied "in-house" so long as they pay through smaller front-line forces. Also, the claim that private contractors become monopoly suppliers depends on the arrangements for future recontracting: contracts for renewal can be subject to competition. There is, however, a more fundamental issue concerned with the limits of military outsourcing.

What, if any, are the limits to military outsourcing? The outsourcing of military support functions is a starting point, but are there opportunities for the outsourcing of combat activities? Here, a key issue concerns the transaction costs of contracting. Contracts have to be written and enforced for a range of unforeseen and unforeseeable contingencies and threats over long periods of time. For example, a contract for a private firm to fight in the Korean War would have required a massive resource commitment and uncertainty arising from the private contractor's response to the intervention of China (e.g., a new contract or withdrawal from the conflict). Also, contracts and performance indicators for private firms can give unexpected and undesirable results. For example, private firms aiming to minimize costs might be reluctant to use their costly assets or they might impose collateral damage and costs on civilians; alternatively, they might have incentives to prolong conflicts. Using private firms in combat roles is highly controversial but economists can identify the problems and costs of contracting (known as transactions costs (Hartley 2011a)). In contrast, state-owned armed forces operate military employment contracts that require their personnel to "obey orders", which includes the obligation to fight as and where required by the state with a willingness to accept substantial net disadvantages of the work in the form of injury and ultimately death. With state-owned armed forces, governments use a special military employment contract that avoids the transaction costs of frequent recontracting for new missions.

Contractor behaviour

A further example of public choice analysis concerns arms firms as producer groups and their behaviour on single-source non-competitive defence contracts. Here, arms firms use their specialist knowledge to shift costs and risks to the government buyer. For example, the UK requires firms to comply with its regulations over non-competitive contracts. The UK regulatory agency for such contracts is its Single Source Regulations Office (SSRO), which determines whether a contractor's costs are allowable. The SSRO has reported a number of cases where firms with single-source contracts have claimed for costs that have been shown to be non-allowable, with profits earned on these costs. Examples include contractors claiming for charitable donations, staff welfare (such as Christmas parties and entertainment), bills for hotels and exhibitions, charges to remedy faulty workmanship, and charges for inflation and learning curves. The SSRO also reduced the baseline profit rates on single-source contracts and recovered £1.3 million from Rolls-Royce on its Hawk jet engine contract over marketing costs and an overstatement of the risk of future cost variation (SSRO 2016b).

Single-source contracts raise questions about the reasons for relying on monopoly suppliers. Typically, single suppliers are selected where there is only one supplier able to deliver the requirement, where there are strong reasons for maintaining a national capability, or for reasons of national security. Again, such reasons have to be scrutinized critically. For example, world markets are often competitive, with sufficient suppliers for competition; the "strong" reasons for maintaining a national capability and for national security need to be explained and costed. National producer groups and their trade associations will obviously support national arms procurement for such reasons.

Industrial strategy: UK warship building

Governments are centrally involved in developing policies to determine the future structure and competitiveness of their national defence industries. For example, in 2016, the UK government published an independent report to inform the development of its National Shipbuilding Strategy as part of the country's industrial strategy. The report focused on ensuring a strong UK naval shipbuilding industry matching the needs of the Royal Navy, maintaining skills and maximizing export opportunities. It accepted the need for building warships in the UK for reasons of national security and national sovereign capabilities. It was estimated that the industry employed 15,000 personnel directly and 10,000 indirectly and that it offered socio-economic benefits, especially in deprived areas of the country. However, it was recognized that more research was needed to identify and value these socio-economic benefits (Parker 2016).

The report found that UK warship programmes have taken too long and were not designed to be export friendly. For example, it took 17 years from contract start to delivery for the Type 23 frigates, and in general each 1 per cent delay in time meant a 0.4 per cent increase in programme costs. The result has been fewer and more expensive ships ordered late and entering service years later than first planned (the Augustine effect: see Chapter 3). The report recognized that the UK warship industry was dominated by BAE and that BAE would be the lead supplier for the Type 26 frigates. However, the report focused on the industrial, competition and export opportunities available from the new generation of the Type 31 general purpose frigate. The new Type 31 frigate is viewed as *not* being a complex and sophisticated warship but as a vessel with export opportunities. It should be a modern, innovative design based on a standard platform using a flexible modular approach and block construction, with blocks built at various UK shipyards. The report recognized that not enough national coordinated effort was focused on the export market for UK warships, and the Type 31 frigate was seen as a potential solution.

The report claimed that there is no precedent for building two first-in-class Royal Navy frigates in one UK location and that a separate lead shipyard other than BAE is required. BAE would be allowed to compete for Type 31 work on combat systems, design support and block building if capacity were available. It was recommended that UK regional shipyards be used to build the Type 31, each yard building fully outfilled blocks as part of its modular construction. The challenge with this approach is the need for a lead shipyard or alliance. The report identified seven UK regional shipyards with entrepreneurial attitudes, enthusiasm to embrace change and flexible skilled labour practices forming competitive yards. The regional yards are located in relatively deprived areas of the UK, but most had no recent experience of building large Royal Navy warships. There are few UK companies with the financial and industrial capacity and capability, expertise and naval shipbuilding knowledge to compete for lead shipyard status.

The Parker Report on the UK National Shipbuilding Strategy is a classic example of the application of public choice analysis. The report recognizes the importance of the new Type 31 frigate in developing the new naval industrial strategy: hence, the contract will be used to implement industry restructuring and reorganization. There will be massive opportunities for action and lobbying by all the agents in the military–industrial–political complex. The Royal Navy will have views about the performance requirements for the Type 31 frigate and exports are unlikely to be dominant in its choices. Producer groups will be active. BAE will bid for lead yard status, but the Parker Report asserts that two new ships cannot be built in one yard.

Other yards will seek to be the lead yard or will offer to form an alliance, which, if successful, will create a new competitive supplier for BAE. Each of the regional shipyards in England, Scotland and Northern Ireland will demand a share of the Type 31 work. Local bids will be supported by trade unions, by local Enterprise Partnerships and regional organizations. Local universities and technical colleges will bid for work training skilled labour and offering apprenticeships. Finally, politicians in each area will demand work for their constituencies. The final outcome is likely to be a political compromise rather than a model of economic efficiency! Capital markets rather than political markets are more likely to lead to an efficient industry structure able to supply internationally competitive warships. For example, capital markets will determine whether one yard is capable of developing two warships, whether there are economies of scale, scope and learning from building two warships in one yard, and whether there are further economies from combining warship building with nuclear submarine building (i.e. allowing Barrow-in-Furness to build warship modules). Capital markets will also select the most efficient lead yard and the most efficient regional shipyards. Otherwise, these complex decisions will be made in political markets and determined by the power of various interest groups in the military–industrial–political complex, with taxpayers funding the outcome.

The costs of wars

Many wars start without any mention or consideration of costs. In some cases, war might not be a matter of choice: it might reflect aggression and invasion or it might be a matter of national pride or national survival. However, the wars in Afghanistan (2001) and Iraq (2003) were different in that they involved some discussion of their likely costs. Public choice analysis provides insights into debates about the costs of conflict and the behaviour of agents in the military–industrial–political complex.

Decisions to go to war involve various dimensions, including political, legal (including UN approval), ethical and military inputs. But conflict has an economic dimension in the form of its estimated and realized costs. Wars are costly and the costs can be massive (e.g., the Second World War). In principle, cost estimates enable policy-makers and voters to make informed choices about conflict and whether war can be viewed as a "worthwhile" investment (do its benefits exceed its costs?). But costs are a relatively neglected aspect of conflict. Typically, governments are reluctant to provide estimates of the costs of conflict for various reasons.

(i) Security reasons: official cost estimates provide useful information to an enemy of possible force deployment and conflict duration.

(ii) Uncertainty reflecting the scale, duration, losses and outcome of any conflict.

(iii) Where national survival is threatened, society might be willing to pay any price (e.g., the UK in 1939/40).

(iv) A desire not to deter voters: underestimating costs gains political support for a conflict.

(v) Once an apparently "cheap" war is started, it will be claimed that further funding cannot be refused when a nation's troops are in battle.

At the start of any war of choice, interest groups of politicians, armed forces and defence departments will seek to avoid revealing any cost estimates. Where cost estimates are released, they will inevitably be optimistic and "too low". For example, when the UK was in the early stages of its involvement in the Afghanistan conflict (2001), the electorate was told that the initial troop deployment was sent as a provincial reconstruction team focusing on improving dialogue between the local warlords and politicians. Later, in 2006, when further UK troops were being deployed, there was an official announcement that "we hope to leave Afghanistan without firing a single shot". The reality was drastically different. When the UK ended its involvement in the Afghanistan war, it had suffered 453 deaths of military personnel and UK military budget costs were estimated at some £24 billion for the period 2001–15; other cost estimates were much higher, at £40 billion (Ledwidge 2013).

For the Iraq War, the US initially estimated its costs at under $60 billion, with some estimates suggesting that the war might pay for itself (2002 prices). Early estimates were based on optimistic assumptions that US forces would be welcomed as liberators, that resistance would be limited and that the Iraqi state would remain intact. An alternative estimate suggested a figure of $200 billion but this was dismissed by the Department of Defense. Later, in 2015, it was estimated that the Iraq War had cost the US $815 billion with the Afghanistan conflict costing a further $686 billion, giving an aggregate

US total for both conflicts of $1.6 trillion by 2015. Recent estimates suggest US budget costs for these conflicts of $4.8 trillion (Bilmes & Stiglitz 2011; Crawford 2016). The experience of the UK was similar, with the first estimates of UK military budget costs for its involvement in Iraq of some £1 billion (2009/10 prices). The final UK military costs for the Iraq conflict totalled some £10 billion over the period 2002–10. The aggregate UK military costs for both the Afghanistan and Iraq conflicts was some £35 billion (Hartley 2011b, 2016).

Cost estimates are fraught with difficulties. Costs might be accounting costs or economic resource costs, total or marginal costs using different price bases, and they might refer to Iraq only or include Afghanistan, Syria, Pakistan and US Homeland Security. Costs might be military budget costs for the conflict or include the costs of peacekeeping operations post-combat as well as reconstruction costs. For the US and the UK, real resource costs should include the value of human lives, reflected in deaths and injuries for US and UK military personnel. There are further costs of conflict in the form of the deaths and injuries of Afghan and Iraqi military and civilian personnel and the costs of rebuilding their capital stock of infrastructure, buildings, factories and housing.

Whatever the basis of costs, they are substantial and conflict is not cheap. The resources used in conflict have alternative uses in such forms as hospitals, roads, schools, care for the elderly or lower taxes. A more controversial suggestion would have allowed the payment of a bribe to Saddam Hussein to leave Iraq and for compensation to be paid to Iraqi citizens, still leaving US taxpayers better off.[2]

Conclusion

Public choice analysis appears to offer major insights into the operation of political markets, including the military–industrial–political complex. However, appearances are deceptive and are no substitute for empirical testing. Public choice models offer various predictions that remain to be tested. Further criticism has focused on the use of unrealistic assumptions in relation to voters and their preferences and bureaucracies as budget-maximizers. Nonetheless, the analysis contributes to further understanding of the arms market. It is also useful in analysing the behaviour and response of armed forces, defence departments and arms producers to major external shocks such as disarmament and the challenges of conversion, which are explored in the next chapter.

Notes

1. An example occurred in the 2016 UK referendum on membership of the European Union. The outcome was a vote for Brexit but without any clear indication of the real meaning of Brexit.
2. For example, assume that at the start of the Iraq conflict it was estimated to cost the US $100 billion. As an alternative to conflict the US could have offered Saddam Hussein and his family a bribe of, say, $25 billion to leave Iraq and go into exile; a further $50 billion of compensation could have been paid to Iraqi families; and the US taxpayer would have been better off by $25 billion. Critics would complain that there would be precedents for other dictators and that there would be no guarantees that an exiled dictator would not return after taking the bribe. In defence of such proposals would be the avoidance of war and its costs for all parties.

9

DISARMAMENT, CONVERSION AND PEACE

Introduction

Critics of arms spending focus on the economic benefits of disarmament and the prospects of a peace dividend. There are, of course, other non-economic benefits of disarmament, namely, peace itself and the creation of a safer world. Defence and peace have a common feature in that both are public goods. My consumption of peace is not at the expense of your consumption of peace, and once provided, peace is available to everyone (known as non-rivalry and non-excludability).

A recent experience of major disarmament occurred with the end of the Cold War in 1991.[1] The US and the former Soviet Union, and their associated military alliances (NATO, the Warsaw Pact), ended their Cold War arms race and made major reductions in their arms spending. The result was a new security environment with prospects of a peace dividend from reduced arms spending. Was such a peace dividend achieved? How large was it? And what were the problems in realizing a peace dividend (Gleditsch 1996)?

The economics of conflict: the case for disarmament and peace

The costs and consequences of conflict provide the mirror image of the case for disarmament and peace. Peace allows the successful development of capitalist market economies and other types of economy. A starting point for analysis requires consideration of the impact of wars on market economies. In peace time, these rely on the price mechanism to allocate scarce resources to promote beneficial trade and exchange both within and between nations. Voluntary trading is beneficial to both buyers and sellers, with markets promoting creative power reflected in the growth of output (i.e. more goods and services).

Wars use military force to reallocate resources from losers to winners (cf. theft). Wars arise where a nation uses military force to acquire resources owned by another nation (e.g., land, water, oil, minerals), or they might arise from national pride, or from prejudice, a desire for revenge or from mistakes. Conflict destroys markets, leading to chaos and disequilibrium with a focus on destructive power and society becoming worse off. Wars result in the death of and injuries to military and civilian personnel on both sides, as well as the destruction of military and civilian infrastructure and housing (roads, bridges, hospitals and schools) and the loss of freedoms for the defeated nation. The Second World War is a classic example, with large-scale deaths and injuries of military and especially civilian personnel and the enslavement of the occupied European and Asian territories. Estimates suggest that more than 60 million people were killed, especially in Germany, Japan and Russia, although such estimates are controversial and unreliable.

Further significant costs of conflict arise from enslavement of the conquered nations, with the loss of freedoms, rights and personal liberty. These costs are often ignored but they are nonetheless real economic costs. Conquered peoples and territories lose all national sovereign rights: they might be subject to slavery, forceful relocation of labour to foreign countries, arbitrary arrest and imprisonment, and starvation (e.g., occupied Europe, especially the Netherlands, in the Second World War). Such costs are rarely valued, mainly because there is no obvious method of measuring and valuing them. Possible measures might be developed from economic estimates of the value of life or from the use of measures of quality-adjusted life years (QALYs) or from work on the economics of slavery. Much more research is needed for the development of an appropriate measure of the costs of enslavement in occupied nations. But difficulties of measurement cannot justify the failure to include such costs in estimating the true costs of conflict.

Conflict also promotes technical progress. It leads to the development of new weapons. Examples from the First World War include submarines and tanks and the emergence of a completely new form of warfare: namely, aircraft and aerial warfare. The Second World War resulted in the development of radar and electronic warfare, aircraft carriers, the jet engine, rockets and nuclear weapons. The Korean War and the Vietnam War resulted in the development of helicopters (e.g., for rapid transport of injured military personnel). Some of these military technologies were applied to civilian fields, such as the development of jet airliners, civilian helicopters, space rockets and satellites. There are further developments of new technology in medical science reflected in the treatment and survival of injured military personnel (e.g., survival rates for soldiers injured in the recent Afghanistan and Iraq conflicts). However, such technology benefits of conflict need to be assessed critically. There is the counterfactual of what would have happened to technical progress in the absence of conflict. For example, firms in peacetime would allocate R & D resources to developing new technologies to meet expected future consumer demands, including medical care. Peace avoids the costs of conflict and offers the prospect of a peace dividend.

The peace dividend

The topic of a peace dividend is the focus of some simplistic views of the workings of market and planned economies. The most simplistic view was that disarmament automatically produced a peace dividend since resources were immediately transferred from the military to the civilian economy. This view resembled that of transferring money from one pocket to another. Reality is different. Resource transfers take time and involve costs, known as adjustment costs. We do not live in a world of magic wand economics in which resources are transferred instantly and costlessly from the military to the civilian economy. Transferring resources from military to civilian use is a slow and costly process, involving unemployment and underemployment of resources. Some labour resources released from the military–industrial complex might become unemployed for a period of time before finding a new job that might require retraining or moving to a new location. Former military plant might also remain unused until a new buyer is found with the entrepreneurship and finance to move into new activities, none of which is costless. In some cases, adjustment costs might be so great that reallocation might not be worthwhile and the former military plant and resources will be abandoned to become the modern equivalent of historic medieval castles and former religious abbeys (e.g., used as tourist attractions).

To understand the adjustment process, distinctions are needed between adjustments for the armed forces and for arms industries forming the military–industrial complex. The armed forces and arms industries each employ scarce resources of labour, capital and land with their associated technologies. The armed forces require personnel, equipment, bases and facilities for their air, land and sea forces. Air forces require air bases and flying training areas; armies require garrisons, accommodation and land for training; and navies require ports, docking and repair facilities providing easy access to the sea. Similarly, arms industries require personnel, machinery, equipment, plants and land for development, production, repair and maintenance activities. Some of the activities of both the armed forces and arms industries might lead to pollution of their local land areas, resulting in major clean-up costs when bases and plants are closed (e.g., nuclear, chemical and biological weapons facilities; fuel spillages).

A further distinction is needed between stocks and flows of resources. Reductions in arms spending affect both stocks and flows. Armed forces and arms industries will experience a reduction in demand for their outputs and services, and they will respond with job losses in the short run or the immediate period, followed by base and plant closures over a longer period; in these ways they will reduce their stocks of resources. Resource flows will also be affected since reduced arms spending will signal changing demands for armed forces and arms industries. The military–industrial complex will no longer be an attractive employment and profit opportunity, which will affect flows of labour and capital into these sectors.

Table 9.1 shows examples of reduced arms spending between 1991 and 1995 for some major arms spending nations in NATO and the Warsaw Pact. The data for 1992 and 1995 compared with 1991 are designed to show the speed of adjustment over the short and long term. Often, there are lags in reducing arms spending, reflecting immediate and continued contractual commitments as well as the opposition of interest groups to reduced budgets; but over time, contractual commitments can be changed. On this basis, the stocks and flows distinction can be viewed in terms of contractual commitments and the costs and time needed to change contracts (i.e. to recontract). Interestingly, the socialist command economies in the table experienced much greater percentage reductions in arms spending than the market economies of the US and NATO. Furthermore, the size of the reductions in arms spending between 1991 and 1995 indicates the potential magnitude of the peace dividend (valued at $326,748 million in 1995 for the nations shown in the table). An alternative valuation of peace might be based on estimates of the costs of war and conflict. For example, the financial costs to the US of its involvement in conflicts in Afghanistan and Iraq has been estimated at some $4–6 trillion, and these are US financial costs only, excluding the costs imposed on Afghanistan and Iraq (deaths, injuries, reconstruction and occupation costs for these nations). For the UK, the costs of its role in Afghanistan are estimated to be at least £40 billion by 2020. Such sums would have funded the running of 1,000 primary schools for 40 years or funded free tuition for all students in British higher education for ten years (Ledwidge 2013).

Table 9.1   Examples of arms spending, 1991–95.

Nation	US$ millions, 2014 prices and exchange rates		
	1991	1992	1995
France	69,991	67,789	64,047
Germany	67,596	64,288	53,011
UK	65,413	61,097	53,183
US	487,221	514,822	433,220
USSR/Russia	269,545	57,641	31,342
Bulgaria	1,930	1,459	930
Hungary	2,069	1,999	1,284

Source: SIPRI (2016b).

Understanding the adjustment process for disarmament also requires a distinction between transferable and non-transferable resources. Some resources are readily and cheaply transferred from the military–industrial complex to the civilian economy. Examples are military personnel with civilian skills, such as drivers, computer and IT experts, vehicle maintenance and repair staff, intelligence and security staff as well as aircraft and helicopter pilots. Similarly, industrial personnel working on military jet engines can be transferred to the production of civil jet engines; aircraft production workers can transfer to the motor industry; nuclear scientists can transfer from developing nuclear weapons to working on nuclear power stations; aircraft designers can transfer their design skills to the motor racing car industry; and accountancy and project management skills are also transferable. Capital assets have varying degrees of transferability. For example, military airfields can be converted into civil airports, flying clubs, prisons and industrial trading estates; military accommodation can be used for housing civilians; former military bases in city centres can be used for building new offices and housing; and some defence industrial plant has potential alternative civilian use, such as aircraft plants and dockyards.

However, not all military resources are transferable: some are highly specific to defence activities and have no alternative use value. Examples include military personnel trained to operate missiles, tanks and submarines; paratroopers; repair staff trained to maintain specialized military equipment; and front-line infantry personnel. Some military capital assets are also nontransferable. Military storage facilities for nuclear weapons and ammunition, industrial plant that develops and produces nuclear weapons, and facilities for the development and production of nuclear-powered submarines are all examples of military capital assets that have little alternative use value in the civilian economy. In the limit, these capital assets use land that has alternative uses for, say, farming, housing and industrial buildings, but transferability involves clean-up costs to make the site safe for alternative civilian uses. In some cases, the environmental clean-up costs are massive, as in the case of cleaning up former nuclear weapons research, production and storage facilities.

The adjustment costs and the time required to reallocate resources from military to civilian uses following disarmament can be reversed for the alternative scenario of rearmament. A shift to rearmament is not instant and costless. For example, rearmament in the UK prior to the Second World War started in 1934, continued to 1939 and was extended to about 1944. Under rearmament, existing arms producers expanded capacity, which involved new plant and equipment and the training of new workers. Completely new firms entered the arms industry, including motor car companies that created and managed "shadow factories", which were privately owned and subsidized by the government. Shadow factories produced aircraft, aero-engines and aircraft parts (e.g., Castle Bromwich, West Midlands, initially managed by Lord Nuffield, produced Spitfires and Lancaster bombers). The armed forces also had to be expanded, which required more military personnel, more equipment and more bases. Conscription was used to increase the numbers of military personnel, which required a massive training programme. New technology required new skills: for example, the expansion of RAF Bomber Command involved new aircraft, which required new navigation skills, more airfields and more aircrews. The increased demand for military personnel meant new demands for civilian labour, which were met by an increased supply of women in the labour force. In other words, rearmament takes time and involves costs in shifting from a peacetime economy to a war economy.

Rules for achieving a successful peace dividend

The end of the Cold War was a unique disarmament process. It did not follow a period of armed conflict, as occurred at the end of both World Wars. It was further distinguished by major political, economic and social change in the former Soviet Union and the Warsaw Pact nations of central and eastern Europe, with a shift from centrally planned to market economies (e.g., the break-up of the former Soviet Union, the end of the Berlin Wall, the end of communism in the Warsaw Pact nations).

A United Nations study outlined some economic principles for disarmament (UNIDIR 1993). Three principles are especially important. First, disarmament can be viewed as an investment process involving both costs and benefits. Costs arise from the need for a major reallocation of resources from the military–industrial complex to civilian production. As a result, the economic benefits of disarmament are likely to be small in the short term but much greater in the long term, as resources are allocated to producing a greater output of civil goods and services. On this basis, the economic aspects of disarmament resemble an investment process involving present or short-run costs and future or long-run benefits.

Second, if disarmament is viewed as an investment process, the challenge for any society is to maximize the social rate of return from disarmament.

This requires that reductions in arms spending should be gradual and pre-dictable, occurring in an expanding economy with government policies to assist resource reallocation, so allowing for smooth economic and social adjustment to disarmament. In contrast, consider a scenario of sudden, unexpected and large reductions in arms spending occurring in periods of economic recession and high unemployment and where adjustment is left to market forces where markets are failing to work properly. This scenario is likely to result in high costs, a long transition time and small economic benefits, yielding a low or even negative return from disarmament (e.g., the example of the former Soviet Union).

Third, there are major economic, technological and environmental con-straints on resource reallocation and the conversion of armed forces and arms industries. Minimizing the costs and maximizing the benefits of disar-mament requires a variety of public policy measures, involving entrepreneur-ship, managerial innovations, financial commitments, manpower retraining, capital tooling and other initiatives, each affecting the armed forces and arms industries. Potential losers from disarmament will oppose change. Examples include localities where military bases and industrial plants are likely to close, involving job losses for military and civilian personnel.

Other barriers to disarmament comprise military units that are sched-uled to be disbanded, military R & D staff and trade unions whose members are likely to be made redundant. In other words, a variety of special interest groups exist that, as likely losers, will oppose disarmament. In some cases, the physical conversion of defence plants and equipment can be difficult and costly, so it might be cost-effective to abandon such specialist plants. A fur-ther aspect of opposition to change and disarmament arises where interest groups might favour conflict. For example, the British army's involvement in Afghanistan was used to justify retaining a larger army (a philosophy of "use them or lose them" (Ledwidge 2013: 120)).

The economics of conversion

Conversion is one aspect of disarmament and it has at least two interpreta-tions. First, there is the narrow interpretation of converting defence plants into plants manufacturing civil goods. This is the swords to ploughshares, tanks to tractors, and submarines to dishwashers approach to conversion. Second, there is a broader interpretation where conversion is viewed as the reallocation of resources from the military–industrial complex to the civilian economy. This section focuses on the narrow interpretation of conversion (UNIDIR 1993).

Critics often claim that arms producers can convert to a variety of civil uses. Reality is different. History shows that private-enterprise market economies have not been successful in converting defence plants to civil markets. After the Second World War, tank factories tried to convert to the production of tractors; but their tractors looked like tanks and failed to sell! There are exceptions where conversion has been successful, such as military aircraft plants producing civil airliners and aero-engines and warship yards producing merchant ships and oil rigs. But are arms producers incompetent and inefficient in failing to exploit the apparently massive opportunities for civil market sales? Why can't and why don't arms firms convert their plants to produce televisions, washing machines, motor cars, fridges, microwave ovens and energy-saving products? Economics explains why such conversions do not occur.

Privately owned arms producers comprise prime contractors who design, develop and produce modern arms as well as suppliers who provide parts and components to prime contractors. Firms in the supply chain can often convert from military to civil production. For example, suppliers of track for tanks can easily adapt their plant and workforce to produce track for earth-moving equipment (bulldozers, cranes), and the manufacturers of helicopter rotor blades can supply similar products for wind farms. But attempts to use skills and plants developed for arms production in civilian areas encounter at least two major problems:

(i) *Conversion is costly*. Costs arise in converting arms plants and retraining the workforce. Some arms plants are highly specialized for weapons production. For example, a large plant designed for the production of large ballistic missiles or nuclear-powered submarines is not the most efficient plant for the production of mobile phones, televisions or microwave ovens. Further costs arise in entering new civil markets. There are search costs in seeking new civil markets and identifying markets that are potentially profitable. Here, it has to be recognized that there are often existing civil firms with established reputations in civil markets that have already exploited any potentially profitable market opportunities (e.g., established manufacturers and suppliers of tractors).

(ii) *Many arms producers are arms specialists with no experience of operating in civil markets: they have a culture of dependence on defence markets rather than a culture of enterprise.*[2] For such firms, successful conversion needs changes in their management culture as well as changes in their production techniques, workforce skills and marketing skills. Selling arms requires that firms respond to the military requirements of their national defence ministry, which specifies its requirements in considerable detail (e.g., a requirement for a fighter aircraft with a specific speed, range and weapons carrying capability). In contrast, a private-enterprise manufacturer of motor cars has to identify consumer demands, raise funds for a new development, and take risks that the new car will sell and earn a profit or incur losses: these firms have to cope with uncertainty.

A simple framework can be used to assess the prospects for converting arms producers to civilian work. Two characteristics are important. First, a firm's dependence on arms sales reflected in its reliance on a single customer, non-competitive cost-based contracts, government-funded R & D, a protected market, guaranteed profits and a culture of dependence rather than one of enterprise. Second, an arms producer's dependence on defence-led and defence-specific technology and assets. Some defence technologies and assets are easily transferable from arms to civil markets. Examples include aircraft, aero-engines, avionics, helicopters and radar; others have few, if any, civil applications, such as stealth technology, armour and nuclear weapons. Table 9.2 provides an analytical framework for assessing the prospects for conversion. Firms in box A are those where conversion is easiest and most likely. In contrast, firms in box D face the greatest difficulties of conversion: they are highly dependent on arms sales and on defence-led and defence-specific technology and assets (i.e. where transferability is most difficult and costly). The framework combines both technology and physical and human capital assets to show the relevance of physical plant and equipment as well as human capital and highly specific skills. The framework is meant to be an illustrative guide and requires more detail, such as the definition of high and low. For example, high sales dependency might be firms that are 80–100 per cent dependent on arms sales while low might be arms firms that are only 10–20 per cent dependent on arms sales.

Table 9.2   A framework for conversion.

		Dependence on arms sales	
		Low	High
Dependence on defence-led and	Low	A	B
defence-specific technology and assets	High	C	D

Specialist arms firms wholly dependent on arms business will find direct conversion technically difficult, costly and probably not worthwhile. Their culture, plant, equipment, technology, managers and workforce are highly specific to arms and non-transferable at reasonable cost. In these circumstances, it is probably most efficient to close the specialist arms plant and, if there are willing buyers, redevelop the land for other uses such as housing, industrial estates or shopping centres.

When analysing conversion, a further distinction is needed between privately owned and state-owned firms. Privately owned firms have to satisfy their shareholders by achieving profitable sales. Their conversion will be based on market forces, reflecting the costs of conversion and its expected profitability: such conversion might be classed as market based. State-owned enterprises are different in that they are owned by governments and will pursue objectives other than maximum profits; they might be monopolies protected from competition; and they might be subject to "soft" budget constraints. Conversion for state-owned firms might involve firms selecting new options for their business with little regard for market forces. For example, state-owned fighter aircraft plants might decide to develop new civil airliners or new light aircraft as a means of utilizing their labour and capital resources. Such conversion might be successful in maintaining employment but not in terms of producing, say, a successful new light aircraft that actually sells and earns profits. This conversion might be classed as supply-side conversion: it needs continuous supplies of government finance to survive and there are likely to be better alternative uses of scarce resources.

While the focus of this section is on arms industries, similar problems and opportunities exist for the conversion of the resources used by the armed forces. There is, however, a major difference with private industry. The armed forces are owned by the state and usually there are no equivalent of private firms in the military (i.e. military units are not organized as private firms exposed to competition, profitability and capital markets). However, the conversion problems for the armed forces are similar to those facing arms producers. The armed forces comprise labour and physical capital resources, including technology and land, each with varying degrees of transferability (see Table 9.2). Redundant military bases might have alternative uses: military accommodation could be used for housing civilians, military sports facilities can be used by civilians, and military vehicles have civilian uses. But not all military bases have alternative civilian uses: some are highly specific and specialized for military uses, such as missile sites and storage facilities for nuclear weapons. However, the land for such bases has alternative uses, but at a cost (e.g., agriculture, recreation, housing, nature conservation areas).

A review of the long decade of disarmament from the mid 1980s to the late 1990s concluded that the expectations of major economic benefits from disarmament had not been met: expectations of a big peace dividend proved illusory (Brzoska 2007). Resource reallocation from the military sector to the civilian economy was most successful in the expanding Western economies, especially the US. It was least successful in the former socialist countries, where economies contracted. Where resources were scarce (e.g., land), they found alternative uses; but where they were abundant, or where investment for civilian uses was high, they were abandoned (Brzoska 2007: 1205).

Can arms producers be controlled?

Can governments exert any control over their national arms producers? The answer is yes, but governments have to decide what their objectives are and why they wish to control arms producers. Economists have expertise in addressing such questions.

Government controls of arms producers can be multilateral or unilateral. International agreements can impose limits on the levels and types of arms spending. For example, various governments might agree to reduce arms spending and limit certain types of arms spending (e.g., on nuclear, chemical and biological weapons), or to limit arms spending in certain regions of the world (e.g., the Antarctic, outer space), or to limit arms sales to specific countries (e.g., as part of sanctions regimes). International agreements have to be verified and policed to prevent non-compliance, and such monitoring involves costs. International agreements also provide incentives for substitution, as nations replace controlled spending with equipment not subject to controls. Examples include conventional weapons replacing controls on nuclear weapons and submarines replacing restrictions on the numbers of surface warships. Nor can it be assumed that all nations will sign an international agreement: some might not participate in the international control regime and there are always possibilities of illegal trading. Further problems arise where scientists are internationally mobile and can offer their services to any nation, so enabling the transfer of valuable knowledge and ideas and leading to the emergence of new arms producers.

National governments can also control their national arms producers. Controls are wide ranging and include restrictions on factor inputs, prices, profits and exports. For example, there might be limits on an arms firm's R & D spending, or on its advertising, marketing and lobbying expenditures. Or there might be restrictions on arms exports to specific countries or on the type of arms that can be exported (e.g., US restrictions on the export of F-22 aircraft, or export sales of Apache attack helicopters without its Longbow radar). Economic models show that arms producers will respond and adjust to such controls. They can substitute between various factor inputs (e.g., sales staff might replace restrictions on advertising and marketing expenses) or they might export civil airliners and helicopters that can readily be converted into troop transports. Also, there might be unexpected outcomes. For example, the advanced FN rifles manufactured by the arms company FN Herstal, which is owned and regulated by the Walloon regional government of Belgium, are appearing in the hands of jihadists!

National governments can exert further controls on arms producers by cancelling major projects. Opponents of the arms industry often focus on the need to cancel large-scale and costly projects, such as a major combat aircraft, a new aircraft carrier or a replacement nuclear deterrent system. An example is the UK's decision to replace its Trident submarine-based nuclear deterrent force. Critics claim that the Trident replacement would be costly, at some £205 billion, and that it serves no useful military purpose.

Supporters claim that the Trident replacement provides civilian jobs, including highly skilled and well-paid jobs, many in deprived areas offering little alternative employment. Again, critics reply that the money saved by not replacing Trident could be used for new investment that would create many more jobs and enable the regeneration of areas such as Barrow-in-Furness, where the submarines are built.

Points made by critics and supporters illustrate some of the arguments surrounding major costly arms projects. Economists can contribute to the debate by identifying myths, emotion and special pleading: they can subject the various arguments to economic analysis, critical evaluation and seek any available evidence. For example, in the UK Trident replacement debate, the focus on its total estimated costs is misleading since these costs are distributed over the life of the project, estimated at some 50 years: they would not all become available immediately as a windfall gain if the project were cancelled. Jobs arguments need to be assessed carefully. A Trident replacement is about providing peace, protection and security for UK citizens and not about providing jobs and protecting the UK submarine industry. Nor can it be assumed that cancellation would lead to increased public spending in deprived areas: governments, not special interest groups, will allocate public spending. Government choices are much more complex than the apparently simple claims by critics and supporters of major arms projects (CND 2016; Hartley 2012a).

Measuring peace

Specific arms projects are presented as contributing to or against world peace. A global peace index is available to measure a country's peacefulness. The index reflects domestic and international conflicts and the numbers of deaths from conflict. The index is based on 163 nations covering 99.7 per cent of the world's population, and it uses 23 qualitative and quantitative indicators. It allows an assessment of changes in peacefulness and violence over time, and for 2015/16 it concluded that the world was slightly less peaceful than in the previous year. The 2016 report estimated the costs of violence at 13.3 per cent of world GDP, equivalent to $13.6 trillion (GPI 2016).

The 2016 report identified the most peaceful and least peaceful nations in the world. The five most peaceful nations were Iceland, Denmark, Austria, New Zealand and Portugal (in rank order with Iceland number one). In contrast, the five nations at the bottom of the 2016 global peace index were Somalia, Afghanistan, Iraq, South Sudan and Syria (listed in rank order with Syria at the bottom of the list). Europe was identified as the most peaceful region in the world, while the Middle East and North Africa were the least peaceful regions (GPI 2016). Some country rankings are interesting. Sweden was ranked 14th, Germany 16th, the UK was 47th, the US was 103rd, China was 120th, Russia was ranked in 151st place and Syria was bottom, at 163rd (GPI 2016). These rankings are intuitively plausible, which increases their acceptability.

In contrast to peace, there is a global terrorism index based on 162 countries that measures the opposite of peace: namely, conflict.[3] The index estimated that terrorism reached its highest level in 2014 and was mostly concentrated in three nations: Syria, Iraq and Nigeria. The direct costs of terrorism were estimated at some \$53 billion in 2014, with the additional indirect costs of preventing terrorism estimated to cost a further \$117 billion. Two groups accounted for some 50 per cent of terrorist deaths, namely, Boko Haram and IS. Terrorism was closely associated with political violence committed by the state and by the existence of a broader armed conflict. However, the data need to be placed into context. Globally, thirteen times as many people are killed by homicide than die by terrorist attacks (GTI 2015).

Conclusion

Arms producers respond to changes in the demand for arms. They expand during wars and conflicts and contract during peacetime and disarmament. However, if governments expect future threats and conflicts, they will face the challenge and costs of maintaining arms industries during peacetime. Here, possible policy options include placing small-scale orders to retain capacity, "mothballing" capacity, or encouraging arms firms to diversify into related civil markets (e.g., military aircraft firms entering civil aircraft markets). This raises questions about the future of arms producers.

Notes

1. The Cold War lasted from 1947 to 1991, when the former Soviet Union collapsed. An alternative end date is based on the fall of the Berlin Wall in 1989.
2. This was revealed to the author on a visit to Moscow in the early 1990s when interviewing a group of defence managers. They were discussing the problems of conversion. Their attitude was that they would convert only if the government would tell them what to do! They had not adjusted to the fact that market economies are based on a culture of enterprise and entrepreneurship.
3. Data on wars are also available from the Correlates of War Project (COW 2016).

10
THE FUTURE OF ARMS INDUSTRIES

Introduction: do they have a future?

Arms producers and industries will survive so long as nation states face threats to their existence. Threats can be internal through civil wars, rebellions and terrorism or external through other nations or external groups threatening the existence of a nation state. As one expert has stated: "War has always been with us as a violent method of resolving disputes... The history of the world is primarily the history of war" (David 2009: 8).

Over time, wars have been fought between tribal groups, cities, regions and nation states. Conflicts have been of varying durations, ranging from days to years. There have been different causes, including conflict over resources, with wars to change the allocation of resources between different owners: examples include wars over land, mineral resources and water resources. Conflicts have also arisen over national borders, from longstanding grievances and for reasons related to race and religion, including ethnic cleansing. Personal factors can intervene in the form of a desire to remove dictators, protect the weak and a desire for revenge and conquest, and there is also the possibility of war due to mistakes and miscalculations. Political systems are relevant, with democracies dependent on voter preferences for conflict while totalitarian systems and dictatorships can ignore such preferences. Interestingly, the end of the Cold War has not meant the end of wars. Since 1991 there have been conflicts in Afghanistan, Iraq, Georgia, Chechnya, Yugoslavia,

Kosovo, Crimea, Ukraine, Yemen and Syria. Also, by 2017, there were signs of the re-emergence of the Cold War nuclear arms race between Russia and the US.

There is also the concept of the just war originally associated with Thomas Aquinas, which specifies the criteria under which war is morally justifiable, namely, where it is morally right to use armed force, and how the war should be fought. For example, the Allies in the Second World War believed that they were fighting a just war against Hitler and Nazi Germany. The just war concept has been extended to deal with the end of wars and the prosecution of war criminals. At the opposite extreme to war is the concern with peace, reflected in the prophet Isaiah's desire for swords to be turned into ploughshares. This desire for peace has been reflected in various efforts to agree treaties and international agreements aimed at preventing wars and controlling the behaviour of states at war. Examples include treaties on banning the use of chemical and biological weapons and land mines, rules on the treatment of prisoners, and the International Criminal Court at the Hague which tries cases of genocide, war crimes and crimes against humanity. Despite various treaties, the fact remains that wars have not disappeared. However, there is a view that the long-term historical trend is for violence to decline (Pinker 2011).

Generations have been exposed to war. Between 1500 BCE and 1860 CE, there was an average of thirteen years of war for every one year of peace (David 2009). Over time, weapons of war have changed dramatically. Technical change resulted in slings and stones being replaced by muskets, rifles, castles and cannons; cavalry being replaced by tanks and attack helicopters; sail-powered warships being replaced by aircraft carriers and nuclear-powered submarines; and observation balloons being replaced by jet-powered combat aircraft, drones and space satellites. Today's war technology is based on computer-guided weapons with intercontinental range and the development of automated battlefields. Nuclear weapons make war even more unthinkable and undesirable, creating pressures to regulate wars and make them less brutal. Critics of war favour international disarmament, a ban on all war and on specific types of weapons (e.g., chemical, biological and nuclear weapons). This is where economists make a distinction between normative and positive statements. Normative statements are based on beliefs about *what ought to be,* such as ideal states of the world reflected in a desire for a totally peaceful world without any weapons and warfare. In contrast, positive statements are about *what is,* such as continued external threats to the existence of nation states or the predicted economic consequences of war and peace. All too often in controversies about arms industries, normative and positive statements are not carefully identified and distinguished.

Future threats

The persistence of external threats to a nation's security and existence means that armed forces are required for the self-defence and protection of its citizens, their property, their freedoms and their national interests. Threats take many different forms, some of which are predictable while others are unknown and unknowable. Uncertainty means that no one knows the form and origin of threats some 20–50 years ahead. For example, in 1941 the US was unprepared for the attack by Japan on Pearl Harbour, and in 2001 it was also unprepared for the Al Qaeda terrorist attacks on New York's twin towers. These were contrasting attacks by a nation state and by a small terrorist group, respectively, with the terrorist group mounting an effective aerial attack without possessing an air force.

The continued existence of current and future threats to nation states will mean that arms producers and industries will be needed to supply equipment for a nation's armed forces. This does not mean that in the future, arms producers and arms industries will remain unchanged: they will continue to evolve. Their future will depend on national arms spending: more spending means larger arms industries, and disarmament means smaller arms industries. However, a distinction is needed between arms industries and arms producers. Even where arms industries might become smaller, their arms producers could expand and increase in size, creating even more powerful producer interest groups. This chapter explores some possible developments for arms producers that will form future arms industries (an industry comprises a group of similar firms). Inevitably, forecasting the future is fraught with uncertainty and requires the standard health warning: namely, that such forecasts are most likely to be wrong. The future is uncertain and is characterized by unknown unknowns.

A short-term future

The short-term future might be defined as the next five to ten years. Such a period is likely to be a development of present trends, with the continued existence of arms producers in something like their current form and size. The short-term future raises issues about the regulation of arms producers, their performance and whether state regulation might improve performance. Various performance indicators might be addressed, including profitability, international competitiveness, exports, project costs and delays. Each aspect of performance needs careful definition, analysis and evaluation before formulating appropriate policy solutions and recognizing the law of unintended consequences.

For example, concerns about the profitability of arms producers needs to start from a reliable data base and the determinants of arms producer profits. Too often, critics claim that high profits prove that taxpayers are being exploited. The arguments and evidence need to be explained and evaluated. What are "high" profits? How high is "too high"? Why do such profits arise? High profits might be defined in relation to the average rate of return earned by all industry, with returns higher than the national average defined as "high" profits. But such criteria need to adjust for the riskiness of the work, which clearly varies throughout the economy: high profits might reflect high risks. Ownership cannot be ignored. Presumably, high profits earned by a state-owned firm might be viewed as acceptable since the returns accrue to the state and the taxpayer, whereas similar profits earned by a privately owned arms producer might be viewed as taxpayer exploitation, and therefore be deemed unacceptable. But, regardless of ownership, the causes of high profits have to be addressed. High profits earned by a state-owned arms producer might reflect monopoly profits and inefficiency whereas such profits earned by a privately owned competitive firm might reflect short-run abnormal profits that will be competed away by rival firms. Alternatively, high profits for a privately owned firm might result from an inefficient private monopoly. Another possibility is that high profits might reflect wartime orders, as occurred in the First and Second World Wars (Ciccone & Kaen 2016).[1] The policy solutions for high profits are equally diverse. They include the imposition of a maximum profit rate on national arms contracts, changing ownership from private to state ownership, breaking up private monopolies, and/or introducing competition into arms markets (e.g., from foreign firms). During wars, legislation might be introduced to control and tax excess profits by arms producers. Again, there are no costless options: each policy involves both benefits and costs.

To illustrate that all policies involve both benefits and costs, consider the example of changing ownership from private to public ownership. State ownership is not an immediate and panacea solution since it raises a variety of issues that need to be resolved. The objectives of the state enterprise need to be specified (e.g., profitability, employment, growth, exports, etc.). Next, it has to determine its prices, output and profitability (e.g., average or marginal cost pricing). Further problems arise in determining internal and allocative efficiency since state-owned firms are monopoly suppliers lacking the pressures from private capital markets. There are, for example, no external checks on the state firm's choice of inputs, including sales, office and managerial expenses, all of which are funded by taxpayers (e.g., luxury offices, company cars, on-the-job leisure). Instead, the internal efficiency of a state enterprise is usually monitored by government, politicians and civil servants, none of whom are experts at running arms companies and none of whom bear any of the risks of their business decisions. The result is likely to be substantial X-inefficiency. In contrast, privately owned firms, even where they are monopolies, are subject to the external checks of the private capital market, with its threats of takeovers and bankruptcy. Also, over time, rivals can emerge and technology changes, so private monopolies are likely to be temporary. Again, each form of ownership involves benefits and costs and the final choice on the form of ownership will depend on any available evidence on benefits and costs and ultimately on voter preferences (reflecting their subjective judgements). The long-term future of arms producers is much more uncertain.

The long-term future

Do arms firms have a future and, if so, what might their future look like? The long-term future might be regarded as the next 50 years, which is highly uncertain, unknown and unknowable. Nonetheless, there are some knowns that identify the broad parameters of the arms producers of the future.

First, the experience of the last 50–100 years is informative. In 1900, aerospace firms did not exist: there was no BAE Systems, Boeing or Lockheed Martin, nor were there any guided missiles or nuclear weapons. Warfare in the First World War relied on large conventional forces, and aircraft, submarines and tanks were only just emerging. The armed forces adjusted to new technologies, reflected in, for example, the creation of air forces as a completely new military force. In contrast, the Second World War was different, with major roles for aircraft and strategic bombing, submarines and tanks with the early emergence of jet engines, rockets and the atomic bomb. Again, the arms firms of 1945 were radically different from those of 1900 and from those of today. On this basis, it seems likely that the arms firms of 2067 will be as different from today's firms as today's firms are from those of 1945 and 1900.

Second, unless there is a sudden and unexpected emergence of world peace and a guarantee of such peace lasting, nations will continue to require armed forces for their national protection. Even if a new world order based on peace were to emerge, the guarantee of such peace will require some form of United Nations peacekeeping force to enforce and maintain world peace, and such a force will require modern, high-technology arms to achieve its mission. Without such a peaceful new world order, nations will continue to require armed forces for their protection, security and safety. But threats will change: new threats will emerge in different forms and in different parts of the world, as a result of which armed forces and arms industries will need to change. Again, future new threats are likely to be completely different from those of today. For example, after the Second World War the major threat in the Western Hemisphere was represented by the Cold War, which ended in 1991. There followed a series of regional conflicts and the emergence of a new threat in the form of international terrorism, where terrorists used armed forces in the form of ad hoc small groups of volunteer fighters and suicide bombers. National armed forces responded by creating smaller, more mobile forces, by focusing on communications and surveillance, through greater internal security (based on national police forces), and by armed intervention in countries where terrorist groups were based (e.g., Afghanistan, Iraq). Also, new nuclear threats might emerge from terrorists acquiring such weapons, from a renewed nuclear arms race between Russia and the US, and from new nuclear states (e.g., Iran).

Third, arms will continue to be costly and their unit costs will continue to rise (the Augustine effect). Rising costs will mean smaller national markets for national arms producers and smaller armed forces. In effect, economics will result in disarmament. Armed forces and conflict will become costlier and economics predicts that higher costs will mean fewer conflicts (and lower costs means more conflicts).

Fourth, technical progress will lead to more radical changes in arms firms. New technology provides opportunities for new entrants, existing firms will acquire new firms with relevant technology, and firms failing to adjust will exit the industry. For example, military helicopter technology will be advanced, reflecting the realization that the designs of the 1960s to 1980s have reached their design limits. Furthermore, the emergence of UAVs will lead to their substitution for manned aircraft, with the armed forces no longer requiring conventional air bases with long runways; pilot training will change, with ground operatives replacing pilots; and UAVs will require less maintenance and servicing compared with the maintenance requirements of operating manned combat aircraft. With UAVs, private firms might be willing to agree long-term contracts for the guaranteed provision of, say, a specified number of drones to be available per day.

Fifth, arms firms will respond and adjust to changes, new technologies and new threats, leading to new forms of business organization. Private arms producers will always respond to new profit opportunities and new methods of minimizing transaction costs. Changes in the techniques for managing business will lead to changes in the traditional mix of "make and buy", probably with new methods of managing international supply chains or organizing R & D. For example, aerospace firms might shift their production work to overseas suppliers while they focus on high-value-added work such as R & D and project management. Or future arms R & D might be undertaken by small agile teams rather than the current large-scale bureaucratic organization of arms R & D.[2] Arms firms will also search for new business opportunities by moving into, say, security, outsourcing and space markets. They will enter civil markets as a means of diversification and reducing their dependence on arms markets as well as acquiring new production technologies that can be applied to arms production (e.g., experience of large-scale production in the civil aircraft and motor car industries).

There is likely to be a continued trend towards a smaller number of larger arms firms. Initially, this trend will involve *national* mergers and acquisitions, with arms firms acquiring other domestic defence firms and becoming specialist suppliers of a range of air, land, sea and security equipment. There might be some vertical mergers, with arms prime contractors acquiring some of their major suppliers (e.g., aircraft firms acquiring aero-engine and aero-structure firms). More radical structural changes would involve the formation of *international* mergers. Possible examples include mergers between major US arms firms and their European rivals, such as Airbus, BAE Systems and Leonardo. Such international mergers of arms firms would create political and monopoly problems. Nation states might oppose the creation of international mergers, which might be viewed as a loss of independence and national security. National competition and regulatory agencies are also likely to oppose the creation of international arms suppliers because of their monopoly power and the reduced bargaining power of national defence ministries. In both cases, preventing international mergers involves costs, with national independence and national control of monopoly power achieved at a price in terms of lower efficiency and higher costs for the procurement of arms from a national defence industrial base.

Some challenges

Governments and arms producers face many future challenges. These include the following examples:

(i) *Adjusting to unexpected change.* New technology will impact on both the armed forces and arms producers. The emergence of cyber warfare is a good example. Historically, nation states intervened in changing foreign regimes through direct military invasion or by supporting rebel groups committed to overthrowing the ruling government (e.g., military coups). Information was also acquired through intelligence and spy networks, but spies are being replaced by electronic and cyber warfare and by drones. Cyber warfare raises the possibility of using Internet attacks to replace the funding and organization of rebel armies. Cyber attacks enable foreign states to interfere in another nation's democratic election process and to undermine a government (e.g., the US presidential election in 2016). Cyber warfare might also attack a nation's power supply, its banking and financial system, and its military and civil communications systems (Coughlin 2016). Cyber attacks are one example of known changes that will confront armed forces, governments and arms producers, and there will be other unexpected changes to challenge the military–industrial–political complex. Space warfare is one such possibility (the Star Wars scenario).

(ii) *Retaining arms industry capacity*. Social and voter pressures to reduce military spending mean that governments have to address the challenge of maintaining their national arms industrial bases. Traditional thinking on this challenge will have to change. Typically, industrial capacity can be retained by government support for technology demonstrator programmes and by awarding small-scale orders to retain capacity. These are costly options that might not be sufficient to retain the required capacity. Alternatives include the option of mothballing capacity. Mothballing appears to be cost-effective, but appearances are deceptive. Private industry often mothballs some of its plants when faced with a temporary reduction in demand. For example, steel plants are often mothballed while awaiting an increase in demand. Examples of arms industry capacity that might be mothballed include shipyards and aircraft plants and the storing of aircraft jigs and tools (e.g., for US F-22 aircraft). But mothballing is not costless. The mothballed plant has to be maintained and secured, requiring maintenance and policing costs. More importantly, restarting production from a mothballed plant requires a skilled labour force, with all the associated costs of hiring and training new recruits.[3] All nations face this challenge and its solution can be viewed as a collective-action problem. On this basis, a group of nations might choose to support the retention of key arms industry capacity collectively. There would be major challenges in identifying such key capacities, their location and the allocation of costs between member states (burden-sharing issues). The NATO military alliance provides the basis for a collective-action approach to retaining key arms industry capabilities, but NATO has rarely been successful in solving such collective-action problems mainly because of issues of free riding and trust between nations.

(iii) *Rising costs of arms*. Costs embrace both development and unit production costs. Rising costs will mean reduced quantities demanded by each nation's armed forces, resulting in small-scale national orders. Again, collective action is a possible solution: where groups of nations combine their buying power and agree to buy one type of weapon from a single supplier. Reality distorts efficiency when nations demand some work sharing from their orders and equity interferes with efficiency. Collective buying also requires national governments to agree collectively on their buying requirements. Joint buying offers a temporary solution to the challenge of rising arms costs but it does not address the fundamental issue of the underlying causes of such cost increases.

(iv) *Arms producers and unit costs of weapons.* Arms producers are the obvious source of efforts to reduce unit costs. Privately owned firms have incentives to adopt lower-cost solutions for development and production work, recognizing that without such cost reductions they will lose business. Arms firms operating in competitive markets might offer new and innovative solutions to controlling life-cycle costs. Military outsourcing is an example where the scope of outsourcing could be determined by firms rather than the armed forces, allowing firms to identify new and innovative solutions. Similarly, firms might propose the development of cheaper, disposable UAVs capable of being deployed in large numbers to overwhelm an enemy's defences and to replace the costly and complex combat aircraft projects favoured by prime contractors (the concept of swarming UAVs (Giangreco 2016)). Arms firms will also introduce new production methods, such as automation, improved 3D printing and new partnership arrangements with suppliers. New materials such as new forms of stronger composites are emerging from experience of their use elsewhere in the civilian economy (e.g., plastic chairs, soft-drink bottles (Trimble 2016b)). Increasingly, new composite materials will be used in, for instance, primary aerospace structures. These developments offer possibilities for creating new forms of business organization.

(v) *New business organizations.* Arms firms will search for new methods of undertaking business, including the acquisition of new firms able to offer market and cost-reduction opportunities. One possibility involves international mergers of arms firms to create large international arms companies. Both horizontal and vertical mergers are possible, such as airframe firms acquiring helicopter and aero-engine companies. Once the opportunities for *national* mergers have been fully exploited, arms firms will look to *international* mergers. Possible examples would include mergers between major US and major European and Asian arms firms. Furthermore, arms firms seeking new solutions will increasingly explore market and cost-reduction opportunities offered by civil firms. Civil aircraft firms will have experience of large-scale production techniques that might be applied to the production of military aircraft. Similarly, motor car firms have experience of development and production methods relevant to arms production. The acquisition of knowledge about new production techniques does not require the acquisition of new firms in other industries: key personnel can be hired from, say, the motor industry. Also, arms producers with a range of air, land and sea systems businesses can apply new development and production techniques from, say, the aerospace industry to the warship building industry (e.g., stealth technology). But innovation in arms industries requires a government response.

(vi) *Governments need to be innovative in their procurement requirements*. Controlling the trend of rising unit arms costs requires a government response. New forms of contracting will be needed to provide arms firms with incentives to reduce the trend of rising unit costs. Governments will have to be prepared to offer generous profit payments to reward innovation. The prospect of international arms firms emerging will provide further challenges to governments in allowing such mergers and in regulating the new giant companies. Government refusal to allow international mergers of arms firms will involve costs; in such cases, governments will have to be willing to pay the price of national independence.

Conclusion

Arms producers and industries have a future, but they will have to change. They will be larger producer groups and there will be some new entrants arising from new technology. Similarly, technical change will mean the exits of some established producers, continuing a long-run trend of major firms departing the arms industry and moving into other markets or entering bankruptcy. The aircraft industry is a good example of these changes. In its early stages, the industry comprised large numbers of small firms that were inventors, innovators, designers and owners (e.g., Bleriot, Wright Bros, Sopwith (Hartley 2014)). Over time, the original entrants changed, becoming larger firms with large design and development staffs no longer dominated by a single designer and with different company names. By 2017 the major industry names included Airbus, BAE Systems, Boeing, Lockheed Martin, Leonardo and Northrop Grumman. These firms are involved in military aircraft, some have major civil aircraft and helicopter businesses, while others supply arms for land and sea forces. Also, some are suppliers of missiles, rockets and UAVs as well as space systems.

The future arms producer will respond to the massively uncertain requirements of future warfare. For example, warfare in 2017 has departed from the traditional battlefield scenario with conflict between established armed forces. Instead, modern warfare involves conflict with guerrilla and terrorist groups using small arms and unconventional methods and arms (e.g., suicide bombers, hijacked airliners as flying bombs as in 9/11) and advanced surveillance methods; modern arms and nuclear weapons are of little apparent use. Nonetheless, today's armed forces have to be equipped to fight any future war with an unknown enemy using unknown weapons in an unknown location at some unknown future time. Armed forces are not like tap water that can be turned on and off whenever required. Instead, armed forces have to be equipped and trained to use modern high-technology arms.

Overall, arms producers will continue to exist, providing an industrial capability to meet future unknown and unknowable threats that will not disappear. For arms firms, their next major moves may be into electronic battlefields, robots and space, with defence electronics firms dominating the industry. An early development is the use of unmanned drones to attack enemy targets, their operators sitting thousands of miles away in perfect safety. The future might be some version of Star Wars. Whatever the future outcome, the art of war will remain a part of the human story, being a matter of life and death, a road to safety or to ruin (David 2009: 8). It was once said that the US fights its wars by loading massive resources into a conflict, whereas Europe is a continent littered with ruins demonstrating the fallibility of human decisions.

War and arms producers are a field in which economics and ethics are inextricably linked. As this book has demonstrated, economics has a contribution to make in this debate. It has identified the theoretical and empirical contributions that need to be considered in any debate about arms producers. There remains a massive task in continuing to identify the myths, emotion and special pleading that surround arms industries and subjecting them to critical economic scrutiny.

Notes

1. A study of the financial performance of US aircraft firms during the Second World War found that aircraft stocks showed positive abnormal returns during the defence build-up and the start of hostilities, and negative returns at the end of hostilities. The companies accounting returns improved during the war but this was not reflected in higher stock returns for shareholders. Finally, investors could have earned higher returns if they had moved out of aircraft stocks after Pearl Harbour and reinvested in the overall market (Ciccone & Kaen 2016).
2. Examples of new research initiatives include the entry of Space X into the space launch industry, Google's research into UAVs, and Amazon's plans to develop its own drones for home delivery services (Thisdell 2016).
3. Similar problems of retaining capacity during peace time apply to the armed forces. Military capabilities can be retained by maintaining a large peace-time military force, which is costly; or reserve forces can be retained, providing a capability in emergencies; or some equipment can be mothballed and kept ready for use in emergencies; or in emergencies, a nation can rely upon conscription, but then it takes time to create and train a competent fighting force, and conscripts require years of training to operate modern advanced equipment (e.g., combat aircraft).

REFERENCES

AeroSpace and Defence Industries Association of Europe 2014. "Facts and figures 2014". Report. Brussels: ASD.

Augustine, N. R. 1987. *Augustine's Laws.* London: Penguin.

Australian National Audit Office (ANAO) 2016. "Tiger–army's armed reconnaissance helicopter". Report 11. Canberra: ANAO.

BAE 2015. "Annual report 2015". Report. Farnborough: BAE Systems.

Bangert, D. & N. Davies 2015. *Managing Defence Acquisition Cost Growth.* Waterlooville: Polaris Consulting.

Beeres, R. & M. Bogers 2012. "Ranking the performance of European armed forces". *Defence and Peace Economics* 23(1): 1–16.

Behera, L. 2013. *Indian Defence Industry.* New Delhi: Institute for Defence Studies and Analyses.

Bilmes, L. & J. Stiglitz 2011. "The case of the Iraq war". In *Handbook on the Economics of Conflict*, D. L. Braddon & K. Hartley (eds). Cheltenham: Elgar.

Brzoska, M. 2007. "Success and failure in defense conversion in the long decade of disarmament". In *Handbook of Defense Economics*, T. Sandler & K. Hartley (eds), vol 2, 1177–210. Amsterdam: North-Holland.

Campaign Against the Arms Trade (CAAT) 2016a. "Ending the arms trade". Web Article: www.caat.org.uk. London: Campaign Against the Arms Trade.

Campaign Against the Arms Trade (CAAT) 2016b. "Arms to renewables". Web Article: www.caat.org.uk. London: Campaign Against the Arms Trade.

Campaign for Nuclear Disarmament 2016. *Trident and Jobs.* London: Campaign for Nuclear Disarmament.

Chalmers, M. *et al.* 2002. "The economic costs and benefits of UK defence exports". *Fiscal Studies* 23(3): 343–67.

Chase, M. *et al.* 2015. "China's incomplete military transformation". Report. Santa Monica, CA: Rand Corporation.

Chilcot, J. 2016. "Report of the Iraq Inquiry". Report. London: The Stationery Office.

Ciccone, S. & F. Kaen 2016. "The financial performance of aircraft manufacturers during World War II: the vicissitudes of war". *Defence and Peace Economics* 27(6): 745–73.

Correlates of War Project (COW) 2016. "Data sets". Correlates of War Project (website). Available at www.correlatesofwar.org/data-sets.

Coughlin, C. 2016. "Russia is organising a cyber-coup in America", *Daily Telegraph*, 2 November.

Crawford, N. 2016. "US budgetary costs of wars through 2016: $4.79 trillion and counting". Costs of War Working Paper. Providence, RI: Watson Institute, Brown University.

Damodoran, A. 2016. "Financial data". Report, January. New York: Stern School of Business, New York University.

David, S. 2009. *The Encyclopedia of War: From Ancient Egypt to Iraq*. London: Penguin Random House.

Davies, N. *et al.* 2011. "Intergenerational equipment cost escalation". Report. London: DASA–DESA, Ministry of Defence.

Defence Committee 1992. "European fighter aircraft". House of Commons HCP 299, March. London: HMSO.

Dorman, A., M. Uttley & B. Wilkinson 2015. "A benefit, not a burden". Policy Pamphlet. London: King's College.

Downs, A. 1957. *An Economic Theory of Democracy*. New York: Harper Row.

Drew, J. 2016. "B-21 bomber breaks cover for the USAF". *Flight International* 189(5528): 11.

DSTL 2010. "Historical cost data for RAF aircraft, 1935–65". Report. London: Ministry of Defence, using DSTL version.

Edwards, C. & N. Kaeding 2015. "Federal government cost overruns". Tax and Budget Bulletin. Washington, DC: Cato Institute.

Eisenhower, D. 1961. "Farewell address". Speech, January. Washington, DC.

Elliott, C. 2016. "The Chilcot report: early thoughts on military matters". *RUSI Journal* 161(4): 4–7.

European Defence Agency (EDA) 2016. "National defence data 2013–2014". Report. Brussels: European Defence Agency.

Flight 2016. "Powering change". *Flight International* 190(5554): 7.

Freeman, S. 2016. "Special treatment: UK government support for the arms industry and trade". Study. Stockholm: SIPRI (for CAAT).

Giangreco, L. 2016. "Don't blame the Gremlins". *Flight International* 90(5553): 30.

Gleditsch, N. *et al.* (eds) 1996. *The Peace Dividend*. Amsterdam: North-Holland.

Global Peace Index (GPI) 2016. "Global Peace Index, 2016". Report. New York: Institute for Economics and Peace.

Global Terrorism Index (GTI) 2015. "Global Terrorism Index, 2015". Report. New York: Institute for Economics and Peace.

Gray, B. 2009. "Review of acquisition for the Secretary of State for Defence". Report. London: Ministry of Defence.

Harford, T. 2007. *The Undercover Economist*. London: Abacus.

Hartley, K. 1983. *NATO Arms Co-operation: A Study in Economics and Politics*. London: Allen & Unwin.

Hartley, K. 2011a. *The Economics of Defence Policy: A New Perspective*. London: Routledge.

Hartley, K. 2011b. "The costs of conflict: UK experience in Afghanistan and Iraq". In *Frontiers of Peace Economics and Peace Science*, M. Chatterji *et al.* (eds). Bradford: Emerald.

Hartley, K. 2012a. "Options for the UK's nuclear weapons programme: defence-industrial issues". BASIC Trident Commission Discussion Paper. London: BASIC.

Hartley, K. 2012b. "Company survey series: BAE Systems PLC". *Defence and Peace Economics* 23(4): 331–42.

Hartley, K. 2014. *The Political Economy of Aerospace Industries*. Cheltenham: Elgar.

Hartley, K. 2016. "Costs of conflict and deterrence: a UK perspective". *International Journal of Peace Economics and Peace Science* 1(1): 41–52.

Hartley, K. & B. Solomon 2014. "Defence inflation: multi-country perspectives and prospects". *Defence and Peace Economics* (special issue) 27(2): 184–298.

Hartley, K. *et al.* 1997. "Armoured fighting vehicle supply chain analysis". Summary of Report. York: Centre for Defence Economics, University of York.

Hitch, C. & R. McKean 1960. *The Economics of Defense in the Nuclear Age*. Cambridge, MA: Harvard University Press.

House of Commons 1989. "The working of the AWACS offset agreement". HCP 286, House of Commons Defence Committee. London: HMSO.

House of Commons 2016. "Use of UK manufactured arms in Yemen". HCP 928, Parliamentary Committee on Arms Exports Controls, House of Commons. London: The Stationery Office.

Hurley, W. *et al.* 2014. "Use it or lose it: on the incentives to spend annual defence operating budgets". *Defence and Peace Economics* 25(4): 401–3.

International Institute for Strategic Studies (IISS) 2016. "The military balance 2016". Report. London: International Institute for Strategic Studies.

Kirkpatrick, D. 1995. "The rising costs of defence equipment: the reasons and the results". *Defence and Peace Economics* 6(4): 263–88.

Kirkpatrick, D. 2000. "Life cycle costs for decision support: a study of the various life cycle costs used at different levels of defence policy and management". *Defence and Peace Economics* 11(4): 333–68.

Kirkpatrick, D. & P. Pugh 1983. "Towards Starship Enterprise: are the current trends in defence unit costs inexorable?". *Aerospace* 10(5): 16–23.

Kopte, S 1997. *Nuclear Submarine Decommissioning and Related Problems*. Bonn: Bonn International Center for Conversion.

Laffonf, J. & J. Tirole 1993. *A Theory of Incentives in Procurement and Regulation*. Cambridge, MA: MIT Press.

Ledwidge, F. 2013. *Investment in Blood: The True Costs of Britain's Afghan War*. New Haven, CT: Yale University Press.

Lipczynski, J., J. Wilson & J. Goddard 2009. *Industrial Organization: Competition, Strategy and Policy*, 3rd edn. London: Pearson.

Lipsey, R. & K. Chrystal 1995. *An Introduction to Positive Economics*. Oxford: Oxford University Press.

Lorrell, M. 1995. "The gray threat: assessing the next-generation European fighters". Report. Santa Monica, CA: Rand Corporation.

Mathieu, F. & N. Dearden 2006. "Corporate mercenaries: the threat of private military and security companies". Report. London: War on Want.

Minstry of Defence (MoD) 2009. "UK Defence Statistics 2009". London: DASA, MoD.

Moore, R. 2015. "F-111K: Britain's lost bomber". *Air Power Review* 18(3): 10–28.

Morison, M. 2016. "Powering recovery". *Flight International* 190(5562): 36–9.

Mueller, D. 1989. *Public Choice II*. Cambridge: Cambridge University Press.

National Audit Office (NAO) 2011. "Major projects report 2011". HC 1678, NAO. London: The Stationery Office.

National Audit Office (NAO) 2015. "Major Projects Report 2015 and Equipment Plan 2015 to 2025". HCP 488-1, NAO. London: The Stationery Office.

Navarro-Galera, A., R. Ortuzar-Maturana & F. Munoz-Leiva 2011. "The application of life cycle costing in evaluating military investments: an empirical study at an international scale". *Defence and Peace Economics* 22(5): 509–43.

Nuclear Decommissioning Authority (NDA) 2016. "Nuclear provision: the costs of cleaning-up Britain's historic nuclear sites". Report. London: The Stationery Office.

OECD 2016. "Main science and technology indicators 2016". Report. Paris: OECD.

Parker, J. 2016. "An independent report to inform the UK national shipbuilding strategy". Report. London: Ministry of Defence.

Peacock, A. 1992. *Public Choice Analysis in Historical Perspective*. Cambridge: Cambridge University Press.

Peck, M. & F. Scherer 1962. *The Weapons Acquisition Process: An Economic Analysis*. Boston, MA: Harvard University Press.

Pinker, S. 2011. *The Better Angels of Our Nature: Why Violence Has Declined*. New York: Viking.

Pugh, P. 2007. *Source Book of Defence Equipment Costs*. London: Dandy Books.

Rait, P. 2016. "How important were personality, ego and personal relationships to British air–land integration in the Western Desert and Normandy?". *Air Power Review* 19(1): 56–79.

Rich, M. *et al.* 1981. "Multi-national co-production of military aerospace systems". Report. Santa Monica, CA: Rand Corporation.

Romp, G. 1997. *Game Theory: Introduction and Applications*. Oxford: Oxford University Press.

Ruiz, F. *et al.* 2016. "The lobbies' network at the EU policy level: the case of security and defense". *Defence and Peace Economics* 27(6): 774–93.

Sandler, T. & K. Hartley 1995. *The Economics of Defense*. Cambridge: Cambridge University Press.

Sapolsky, H. & E. Gholz 1999. "The defense monopoly". Report. Washington, DC: Cato Institute.

Scherer, F. M. 1964. *The Weapons Acquisition Process: Economic Incentives*. Boston, MA: Harvard University Press.

Shaw, D. 2016. "A miserable damn performance? The effectiveness of American air power against insurgency in Vietnam". *Air Power Review* 19(1): 45–53.

Single Source Regulations Office (SSRO) 2016a. "Annual report and accounts 2015/16". HCP 412, SSRO. London: The Stationery Office.

Single Source Regulations Office (SSRO) 2016b. "Interim compliance statement". Statement, July. London: Single Source Regulations Office.

SIPRI 2015. "Military expenditure data: 1998–2015". Report. Stockholm: Stockholm International Peace Research Institute.

SIPRI 2016a. "SIPRI yearbook 2016". Compendium, Stockholm: Stockholm International Peace Research Institute.

SIPRI 2016b. "Military expenditure database". Stockholm: Stockholm International Peace Research Institute.

SIPRI 2016c. "SIPRI arms transfer database". Stockholm: Stockholm International Peace Research Institute.

Small Arms Survey (SAS) 2003. "Small arms survey, 2003". Report. Geneva, Graduate Institute of International Studies.

Small Arms Survey (SAS) 2015. "Small arms survey, 2015". Report. Geneva, Graduate Institute of International Studies.

Smith, R. 2009. *Military Economics: The Interaction of Power and Money*. London: Palgrave Macmillan.

Theohary, C. A. 2015. "Conventional arms transfers to developing nations 2007–2014". Report. Washington, DC: Congressional Research Services.

Thisdell, D. 2016. "Innovation challenge". *Flight International* 189(5529): 30–31.

Tisdell, C. & K. Hartley 2008. *Microeconomic Policy: A New Perspective*. Cheltenham: Elgar.

Transparency International 2015. "Corruption Perceptions Index 2015". Report. Berlin: Transparency International.

Trimble, S. 2016a. "Fresh delays fuel KC-46A frustration". *Flight International* 189(5541): 19.

Trimble, S. 2016b. "Fantastic with plastic". *Flight International* 190(5557): 30–31.

United Nations Institute for Disarmament Research (UNIDIR) 1993. *Economic Aspects of Disarmament: Disarmament as an Investment Process*. New York: United Nations.

United States Department of Defense (US DoD) 2015. "Selected acquisition reports". Report. Washington, DC.

WMEAT (2016). *World Military Expenditures and Arms Transfers 2015*. Washington, DC: Bureau of Arms Control, Verification and Compliance, US Department of State (available online only).

World Trade Organisation (WTO) 2016. "Compliance report on US challenge to EU aircraft subsidies". Report. Geneva: World Trade Organisation.

Yonge, T. 2013. "A historical perspective on defence procurement: the competition for the replacement of the Avro Shackleton Mk 1 and 2, 1963–1966". *Air Power Review* 16(1): 92–109.

INDEX

Note: bold page numbers indicate figures and tables; numbers in brackets preceded by *n* are chapter endnote numbers.